WALT DISNEY

★ ★ ★ ★ ★ ★ ★ ★ ★ ★ ★ ★ ★ ★ ★

POP CULTURE LEGENDS

WALT DISNEY

★ ★

JIM FANNING

CHELSEA HOUSE PUBLISHERS

New York ★ Philadelphia

CHELSEA HOUSE PUBLISHERS

EDITORIAL DIRECTOR Richard Rennert
EXECUTIVE MANAGING EDITOR Karyn Gullen Browne
COPY CHIEF Robin James
PICTURE EDITOR Adrian G. Allen
ART DIRECTOR Robert Mitchell
MANUFACTURING DIRECTOR Gerald Levine

Pop Culture Legends
SENIOR EDITOR Kathy Kuhtz Campbell
SERIES DESIGN Basia Niemczyc

Staff for **WALT DISNEY**
ASSOCIATE EDITOR Martin Schwabacher
EDITORIAL ASSISTANT Kelsey Goss
PICTURE RESEARCHER Pat Burns
COVER ILLUSTRATION Richard Martin

First Printing

3 5 7 9 8 6 4 2

Library of Congress Cataloging-in-Publication Data

Fanning, Jim.
Walt Disney / Jim Fanning.
p. cm.—(Pop culture legends)
Includes bibliographical references and index.
ISBN 0-7910-2331-1.
    0-7910-2356-7 (pbk.)
1. Disney, Walt, 1901–1966—Juvenile literature. 2. Animators—
United States—Biography—Juvenile literature. [1. Disney, Walt,
1901–1966. 2. Motion pictures—Biography.] I. Title. II. Series.
NC1766.U52D5329 1994   93-27541
791.43'092—dc20   CIP
[B]   AC

FRONTISPIECE:

Walt Disney examines drawings for *Bambi* in 1942.

Contents ★ ★ ★ ★ ★ ★ ★ ★ ★ ★ ★ ★ ★ ★ ★ ★ ★

A Reflection of Ourselves

Leeza Gibbons

I ENJOY A RARE PERSPECTIVE on the entertainment industry. From my window on popular culture, I can see all that sizzles and excites. I have interviewed legends who have left us, such as Bette Davis and Sammy Davis, Jr., and have brushed shoulders with the names who have caused a commotion with their sheer outrageousness, like Boy George and Madonna. Whether it's by nature or by design, pop icons generate interest, and I think they are a mirror of who we are at any given time.

Who are *your* heroes and heroines, the people you most admire? Outside of your own family and friends, to whom do you look for inspiration and guidance, as examples of the type of person you would like to be as an adult? How do we decide who will be the most popular and influential members of our society?

You may be surprised by your answers. According to recent polls, you will probably respond much differently than your parents or grandparents did to the same questions at the same age. Increasingly, world leaders such as Winston Churchill, John F. Kennedy, Franklin D. Roosevelt, and evangelist Billy Graham have been replaced by entertainers, athletes, and popular artists as the individuals whom young people most respect and admire. In surveys taken during each of the past 15 years, for example, General Norman Schwarzkopf was the only world leader chosen as the number-one hero among high school students. Other names on the elite list joined by General Schwarzkopf included Paula Abdul, Michael Jackson, Michael Jordan, Eddie Murphy, Burt Reynolds, and Sylvester Stallone.

7

★ ★

More than 30 years have passed since Canadian sociologist Marshall McLuhan first taught us the huge impact that the electronic media has had on how we think, learn, and understand—as well as how we choose our heroes. In the 1960s, Pop artist Andy Warhol predicted that there would soon come a time when every American would be famous for 15 minutes. But if it is easier today to achieve Warhol's 15 minutes of fame, it is also much harder to hold on to it. Reputations are often ruined as quickly as they are made.

And yet, there remain those artists and performers who continue to inspire and instruct us in spite of changes in world events, media technology, or popular tastes. Even in a society as fickle and fast moving as our own, there are still those performers whose work and reputation endure, pop culture legends who inspire an almost religious devotion from their fans.

Why do the works and personalities of some artists continue to fascinate us while others are so quickly forgotten? What, if any, qualities do they share that enable them to have such power over our lives? There are no easy answers to these questions. The artists and entertainers profiled in this series often have little more in common than the enormous influence that each of them has had on our lives.

Some offer us an escape. Artists such as actress Marilyn Monroe, comedian Groucho Marx, and writer Stephen King have used glamour, humor, or fantasy to help us escape from our everyday lives. Others present us with images that are all too recognizable. The uncompromising realism of actor and director Charlie Chaplin and folk singer Bob Dylan challenges us to confront and change the things in our world that most disturb us.

Some offer us friendly, reassuring experiences. The work of animator Walt Disney and late-night talk show host Johnny Carson, for example, provides us with a sense of security and continuity in a changing world. Others shake us up. The best work of composer John Lennon and actor James Dean will always inspire their fans to question and reevaluate the world in which they live.

It is also hard to predict the kind of life that a pop culture legend will lead, or how he or she will react to fame. Popular singers Michael Jackson

★ ★

and Prince carefully guard their personal lives from public view. Other performers, such as popular singer Madonna, enjoy putting their private lives before the public eye.

What these artists and entertainers do share, however, is the rare ability to capture and hold the public's imagination in a world dominated by mass media and disposable celebrity. In spite of their differences, each of them has somehow managed to achieve legendary status in a popular culture that values novelty and change.

The books in this series examine the lives and careers of these and other pop culture legends, and the society that places such great value on their work. Each book considers the extraordinary talent, the stubborn commitment, and the great personal sacrifice required to create work of enduring quality and influence in today's world.

As you read these books, ask yourself the following questions: How are the careers of these individuals shaped by their society? What role do they play in shaping the world? And what is it that so captivates us about their lives, their work, or the images they present?

Hopefully, by studying the lives and achievements of these pop culture legends, we will learn more about ourselves.

A Funny Feeling

EARCHLIGHTS SWEPT THROUGH THE STARRY NIGHT, while below, the brightly lit theater marquee flashed the title of a brand-new movie making its world premiere. Uniformed ushers lined the sidewalk, greeting the biggest stars of the day as they stepped from the long, sleek limousines. Throngs of fans crowded for a closer view as they applauded and cheered Tinseltown's elite: Cary Grant, Shirley Temple, Jack Benny, Judy Garland, Ginger Rogers, and George Burns and Gracie Allen, among others. The stream of stars showed no sign of slowing.

The scene was the Carthay Circle Theater in Los Angeles, California; the occasion, one of Hollywood's fabled film premieres, a glitzy ritual reserved for only the most important productions rolled out of the factorylike movie studios.

On that balmy night, December 21, 1937, the fans expecting the trappings of a typical Hollywood premiere were not disappointed. But anyone in attendance at this particular premiere was well aware that it was anything but typical.

Holding Donald Duck, Mickey and Minnie Mouse, and a few of the Seven Dwarfs, Walt Disney receives an honorary master of arts degree from Harvard University in 1938.

For the first time in history, Hollywood—and all the world—was awaiting the unveiling of a full-length, *animated* film.

Suddenly flashbulbs popped, reporters lunged forward, and the fans craned their necks as another celebrity arrived. All attention centered on one unassuming but intense man. He, however, was no movie star. A seemingly ordinary fellow, looking uncomfortable in his white tie and tails, he was as famous as any starlet or leading man, as admired as any high-profile director or studio head. This was Walt Disney, and the film that the top names and most influential power brokers in Hollywood were clamoring to see was his creation.

Walt Disney was only 36 years old, but he was already world famous; that very week, millions had seen his photo on the cover of *Time* magazine. A high school dropout, within the year he would be awarded honorary degrees by Harvard and Yale, and he was one of only two Hollywood figures universally regarded as a genius, the other being Charles Chaplin.

Just a few months earlier, Disney had toured Europe, where he was greeted by adoring mobs. He had been welcomed in England by dignitaries ranging from the royal family to author H. G. Wells, and in Italy he had met with dictator Benito Mussolini and the pope. In Paris, Disney had received a medal from the League of Nations (an organization designed to establish cooperation among nations and the peaceful resolution of disputes) that he accepted in the same voice he used to speak the lines of his beloved character, Mickey Mouse, in his popular cartoons.

When Disney had introduced Mickey Mouse in 1928, the animated cartoon was often nothing more than crudely drawn program filler. Less than a decade later, animation had become an art form, and Walt Disney was one of the main reasons why. He had not drawn a picture for one of his own films in years, but his leadership and commitment to quality had attracted a team of superior artists who worked tirelessly to fulfill his vision. With each of the enormously popular Mickey Mouse or *Silly Symphony* cartoons, Disney saw to it that the animation was stronger and funnier, conveying character through more fluid and expressive movement.

When he turned his creative energies toward feature animation, however, the conventional wisdom in Hollywood was that Disney had gone mad. The *Snow White and the Seven Dwarfs* project was branded "Disney's Folly." An hour and a half of loony comic antics and bright colors? No one could conceive of such a thing. No one, that is, except Walt Disney. What he envisioned went far beyond simply lengthening a short cartoon's running time. Disney believed that animation had the

Always a tireless worker, Walt Disney settles behind his desk in February 1933. Only 31 years old at the time, Disney was already the head of a thriving animation studio.

potential to express complex emotions and to tell an intricate, sustained story.

No one knew this better than his own artists. Nevertheless, even they were concerned whether, at a time when the studio was deeply in debt, Disney could risk shifting animators away from producing the profitable shorts that provided his main source of income in order to work on an untried venture whose completion was years down the road. Yet over the objections of Roy Disney, his brother and business partner, Walt had actually expanded his facilities and staff in order to work on his daring new project. In February 1935, a flurry of rumors that the studio would have to be shut down

Walt Disney reviews a musical score with popular singer Nelson Eddy. Behind them is a storyboard for a work in progress starring Willie the Whale. The technique of the storyboard, a rough plan for each shot in a film, was one of many innovations pioneered by the Disney studio.

because of financial difficulties swirled among his employees. Disney called a meeting of the entire staff.

First, Disney surprised his nervous employees by announcing the official commencement of production on *Snow White*. Then, before his amazed audience, he acted out the entire story of the film as he envisioned it. He played every part, creating before their eyes the characters of Snow White, the evil Queen, and the seven lovable Dwarfs, each with his own distinct personality. The troubled mood of his talented artists and technicians was swept away, and his performance was greeted with thunderous applause.

Disney's financial problems were far from over, however. To the alarm of his main creditor, the Bank of America, the film's budget quickly ballooned from a projected $250,000 to $500,000, an amount that made his more financially conservative brother Roy almost apoplectic.

Disney's perfectionism caused further budget problems; he could not resist reworking each scene until it was exactly right. But Disney regretted none of the extra effort and expense. "We've worked hard and spent a lot of money," Disney told a reporter before the premiere. "I've seen so much of *Snow White* that I am conscious only of the places where it could be improved. You see, we've learned such a lot since we started this thing! I wish I could yank it back and do it all over again."

When the feature was finally finished, it had cost $1.5 million—more than twice what even the most expensive live-action picture of the day cost—and every penny was owed to the bank. If *Snow White* failed, there would be no more Walt Disney Studios. "We had the family fortune wrapped up in *Snow White*," was the way Disney put it years later.

It was something of a miracle that the feature was ready to be shown at all. Disney had resolved to complete his film by Christmas; he had made it, but just barely. There were only two prints of *Snow White* in existence, and they had arrived at the theater mere hours before the premiere.

The night before, on famed movie director Cecil B. DeMille's radio program, Disney had confessed to being nervous about the premiere, and small wonder. A sneak preview in Pomona, California, was cause for concern; a third of the audience walked out of the screening. (Only later was it discovered that the walkouts were college students returning to their dormitories before a 10:00 P.M. curfew.)

So it was a distracted Walt Disney who stepped up to the radio microphone that December night before the unveiling of the production on which so much—personally, professionally, and financially—was riding. Disney ably answered the interviewer's questions, but in his nervousness he was unable to name all Seven Dwarfs.

Finally, Walt told the radio audience he was going to watch the screening "and have my wife hold my hand." He escorted Lillian, his spouse of 12 years, into the theater. Soon all the invited guests were seated, the house lights went down, and the screen lit up.

As *Snow White* unreeled, the tuxedoed and gowned audience laughed and applauded. "They even applauded backgrounds and layouts when no animation was on the screen," remembered Ken O'Connor, who was one of the art directors of *Snow White*. "I was sitting near John Barrymore when the shot of the queen's castle above the mist came on. . . . He was bouncing up and down in his seat, he was so excited. Barrymore was an artist as well as an actor, and he knew the kind of work that went into something like that."

Ward Kimball, one of Disney's top animators, recalled that when the grieving Dwarfs knelt before the lifeless Snow White, "everybody in the theater was crying. I couldn't believe it. It was supposed to be just a cartoon and everybody is crying."

When the words "A Walt Disney Production" signaled the end of the movie, this jaded audience of Hollywood insiders and players, many of whom had predicted the project's failure, leapt to their feet, applauding wildly.

Years later, Walt reflected on the experience:

All the Hollywood brass turned out for my cartoon! That was the thing. And it went way back to when I first came out here and I went to my first premiere. I'd never seen one in my life. I saw all these Hollywood celebrities comin' in and I just had a funny feeling. I just hoped that some day they'd be going in to a premiere of a cartoon. Because people would depreciate the cartoon. You know, they'd kind of look down.

I met a guy on the train when I was comin' out. It was one of those things that kind of make you mad. I was out on the back platform—I was in my pants and coat that didn't match but I was riding first class. I was making conversation with a guy who asked me, "Goin' to California?" "Yeah, I'm goin' out there." "What business you in?" I said, "The motion-picture business." "What do you do?" I said, "I make animated cartoons." "Oh." It was like saying, "I sweep up the latrines."

Sometimes people make you mad, and you want to prove something to them even though they mean nothing to you. I thought of that guy on the back platform when we had the premiere of Snow White.

Perhaps Disney thought of that man again when Snow White and the Seven Dwarfs went on to become not only the most popular movie of the year, but one of the most financially successful movies ever made.

2 ★ Memories of Marceline

WHEN ELIAS DISNEY moved his wife, Flora, and five children to a 45-acre farm in Missouri, it was not the first move of his life and it would not be the last. "Pa always had ants in his pants," one of the Disney boys said of Elias. "He could never stay anyplace long enough to warm a seat." In those horse-and-buggy days, it was uncommon for people to move more than 100 miles from their hometown. Yet Elias Disney lived at various times in Canada, Kansas, Colorado, Florida, Illinois, and Missouri, always pursuing the American dream that continually eluded his grasp.

Born in 1859 in Canada of Irish immigrants, Elias moved with his large family—he was the eldest of 11 children—to a farm in Kansas. Elias was restless on the farm and took a series of jobs throughout the country, establishing a pattern he would follow for the rest of his life: when one job did not pan out, he would move on.

Elias returned to the farm when jobs of any kind became scarce. His return was prompted in part by a pretty neighbor girl, Flora Call. Both the Disneys and the Calls, frozen by the Kansas winters, moved to Florida to thaw out

---

Walt Disney's parents, Flora and Elias Disney, are seen here in 1938. Walt's demanding father provided a model of hard work and industry for his ambitious son.

in the southern sun. There, in 1888, Elias married Flora, who had become an elementary schoolteacher.

It was more difficult to say what Elias's profession was; by the time the young couple moved to Chicago with their first son, Herbert, in the spring of 1889, Elias had already worked as a farmer, hotel owner, machinist, carpenter, mail carrier, and soldier. The stint in the military had been an especially short one; Elias had enlisted during a war scare, and when the crisis quickly passed he simply went home, keeping his uniform in lieu of payment.

Chicago was the nation's hub, and the hustling hurly-burly of the enormous city was overwhelming to a country mouse like Elias. Yet he was determined to make a go of his new life. He built his own house, designed by Flora, and began a flourishing carpentry career.

Elias and Flora meshed well. He was sober, upright, and stern; she was patient, understanding, and had a sense of humor. Flora continued to design each house built by Elias, and she also handled the bookkeeping and purchasing.

There were soon two more children to care for, Raymond and Roy. The devout family worshiped at the St. Paul Congregational Church. Flora played the organ and Elias built the new church, and they became friends with the minister, Walter Parr. When the Disneys had another son on December 5, 1901, they named their new child Walter, after their minister.

Almost nine years younger than their last son, Roy Oliver, little Walter Elias was the center of attention. From the start Roy felt a special affection for Walt, pushing his baby brother's carriage and buying toys for him out of his own pocket money.

By the time a daughter, Ruth, came along two years later, Elias was convinced that the increasing crime of Chicago made it an unsuitable place to raise children.

He wanted a wholesome, Christian community for his family, and he found it in the bucolic little town of Marceline, Missouri.

Walt was four years old when the Disney family made the move to Marceline, which is located about 120 miles northeast of Kansas City. To him it was a paradise. His memory of the farm remained vivid years later:

> It was a beautiful farm, with a wide front lawn. Big weeping willow trees. It had two [apple] orchards. . . . One variety was called Wolf River apples, and they were so big that people came from miles around to see them.

The farm was Walt's personal petting zoo. Elias put his youngest son in charge of the pigpen, and Walt rode the largest hogs bareback. He fed a runt named Skinny with a baby bottle, and Skinny followed his young benefactor around the farmyard like a pet dog.

Walt wandered through the pastoral wonderland, soaking up every sensation. The boy learned to wait quietly in the woods, breathlessly watching for rabbits, squirrels, and raccoons. He enjoyed the nuts, persimmons, and wild grapes that grew in abundance. On hot summer afternoons he and Roy splashed in the tranquil

A stereograph from approximately 1900 shows a circus parade marching through Marceline, Missouri, Walt's childhood home between the ages of four and eight. The family farm in Missouri provided Walt with some of the happiest memories of his life.

water of Yellow Creek. The Santa Fe Railroad ran near the Disney farm, and Walt would wave as his Uncle Mike, an engineer, roared by in the mighty locomotive en route to Fort Madison, Iowa.

Walt's first effort at cartooning was a picture of a house complete with smoke billowing from the chimney, drawn on the side of the Disney homestead with a stick dipped in gooey, black tar. His father was so angry about Walt's behavior that he let the tar drawing remain on the wall as a reminder of his transgression.

Like any promising artist, Walt had his patrons. His aunt Margaret supplied him with crayons and fat pads of paper. Old Doc Sherwood, a retired physician living in town, "had this beautiful stallion, Rupert," Disney recalled years later. "Doc had me come over one time and bring my crayons and my big sheet tablet, and I was going to draw a picture of Rupert for him." The delighted doctor paid the young artist a quarter for his handsome drawing.

Elias kept Walt home from school until Ruth was old enough to go, too, so the boy was almost seven before he entered the first grade. Though Flora had taught Walt to read, his grades were only fair; he daydreamed in class and doodled during his lessons.

The neighboring farmers were suspicious of Elias, at first; he had radical notions that did not sit well with the conservative growers. They were skeptical of his socialist ideas, and his efforts to form a farmers' union went nowhere. The neighbors eventually came to like Elias, however, for he was hardworking and community-minded. They also enjoyed his fiddle playing on Sunday afternoons. Walt could only gape during these concerts; his strict father did not seem to him to be the fiddler type.

Elias took his responsibilities as breadwinner seriously—perhaps too seriously. In his grim determination to make the farm prosperous he made heavy demands on

This illustration shows a typical Horatio Alger character, Phil the Fiddler. The popular novelist Alger, a favorite of Disney's as a child, wrote more than 100 books concerning poor boys who achieve success.

his older sons, Herb and Ray. When he ordered them to turn over money they had earned by working at a neighbor's farm, the boys had had enough. Herb and Ray disappeared into the darkness one night, skipping town for Chicago.

Elias was hit hard by the loss of the eldest Disney sons. He came down with typhoid fever, then pneumonia, and the burden of maintaining the farm fell on 16-year-old Roy. It was too much. Flora Disney finally convinced her husband that they must sell the farm. "He had to auction the stock," Walt remembered. "It was the cold of winter and I remember Roy and myself going out and going all around to the different little towns and places, tacking up these posters of the auction." The two brothers sadly stood by as their animals were auctioned off; they cried when their favorite colt was led away by a stranger.

In the spring of 1910, the Disneys headed for Kansas City, Missouri, leaving behind their home in Marceline, the happiest place eight-year-old Walt had ever known. In their new home, Elias Disney once more started from scratch. He bought a distributorship for the *Kansas City Times* and *Kansas City Star* newspapers. Walt and Roy worked as delivery boys for their demanding father. They would arise at 3:30 A.M. to begin work. Walt was personally responsible for some 50 customers.

Snowstorms or rain showers made no difference; the papers had to be delivered. Walt sometimes struggled through snowdrifts taller than he was. In one apartment building's warm hallway, the exhausted boy would sometimes lie down and doze off only to awaken a few minutes later in a panic. For the rest of his life, he had nightmares about failing to deliver his father's newspapers.

Financial troubles left their mark on Elias; he became almost fanatically thrifty, walking miles rather than paying a nickel to ride the trolley. He did not pay his sons anything for their exhausting labors, even though he did pay the other newsboys. Roy, now 19, was fed up with his stern, tightfisted father and his hot temper. In 1912, Roy left for Kansas, where his Uncle Will could always use another hand to help bring in the harvest.

With Roy gone, Elias expected even more of Walt, insisting that he help with carpentry work around the house in addition to delivering his paper route. When

Charlie Chaplin's character, the Little Tramp, was a hero of the young Walt Disney, who acted out Chaplin's comedy routines in amateur performances.

Elias lost patience, as he often did, he whacked the boy with whatever was at hand. It was a frightening situation for young Walt. At 10 years old, he was the only one of Elias's sons left at home, and he bore the full brunt of his father's anger.

Flora Disney helped lighten the gloomy mood with her humor, and Walt delighted in making his mother laugh. He also entertained his little sister. When Ruth was in bed with the measles, he amused her by flipping a series of his drawings so that they seemed to move.

Walt loved to read—Mark Twain, Charles Dickens, and Horatio Alger (a 19th-century author of success stories about hardworking boys who go from rags to riches) were among his favorites—but his grades continued to be unexceptional. Both he and Ruth repeated the second grade; Walt was now almost two years older than his classmates. In art class, he was reprimanded for adding faces to his drawing of a bowl of flowers.

Happily, Walt became close friends with another Walt, Walter Pfeiffer. The young Disney was a constant visitor to the warm, cheerful home of his friend. Walt Disney's father considered entertainment a frivolity, whereas jolly Mr. Pfeiffer knew all the best vaudeville jokes and introduced the wide-eyed boy to an enticing new world of theater and motion pictures.

Aping the acts they saw, the two Walts performed comedy routines at school. They entered amateur nights as "Charlie Chaplin and the Count"; Disney excelled at playing his idol, Chaplin, in the role of the Little Tramp. At school Disney portrayed Abraham Lincoln, complete with pasteboard stovepipe hat and false beard; his recitation of the Gettysburg Address became an annual event on Lincoln's birthday.

Walt sorely missed Roy and looked forward to his brother's visits. Even though Roy lived in Kansas City, where he worked at a bank, the bond between the two remained strong. During one of Roy's visits, Walt's own volatile temper once again clashed with his father's. Knowing what would follow, Roy advised his 14-year-old brother not to take any more beatings.

In the basement, the traditional site for Walt's father to administer a thrashing, Elias raised his hand, but Walt grabbed him by the wrists. Elias struggled to free himself from his son's grip. Tears came to his eyes; he dropped his arms to his sides, and when Walt let him loose, he slowly walked upstairs. Elias never attempted to beat Walt again.

3. Adventures of a Young Cartoonist

AFTER TAKING ONE LOOK AT WALT'S SCHOOL PAPERS, even the most casual observer would have known that Walt Disney was a budding cartoonist. Walt sketched comical animals and characters from the funny papers whenever a piece of paper presented itself. By the time Walt graduated from the eighth grade in 1917, he had made up his mind about his future career: he was going to be a cartoonist.

During this same period, Elias Disney was once again changing his mind about his career. Always on the lookout for a business opportunity that would pay off big, he invested all his savings in a Chicago jelly factory. Because Elias also secured a position as head of construction at the factory, it meant another move for the Disneys.

Elias, Flora, and Ruth packed up for Chicago. Walt stayed behind with Roy and their now-married brother, Herbert; free at last from the hated paper route, Walt looked for a summer job. Roy suggested that Walt work as a railroad "news butcher," selling papers, drinks, and snacks. Walt jumped at

The streets of Chicago are filled with cars and people during a transit strike in 1919. Walt Disney attended high school in Chicago and studied drawing at the Chicago Institute of Art until 1918.

29

the idea; eager to indulge his love of trains and travel, the 15-year-old easily convinced his employers he was the necessary 16 years of age. It was an adventure: he rode the various train lines to six different states and got to wear a snazzy blue uniform complete with a shiny badge and gold buttons. But first he borrowed the required $15 bond from Roy.

A summer of riding the rails and exploring the diverse cities and towns broadened Walt's horizons, but financially it was not a profitable experience. Food and empty bottles were regularly stolen from the young news butcher, and at the end of the summer, Roy did not get his $15 back.

A train pulls into a depot in Valley Falls, Kansas, circa 1910. When he was 15 years old, Walt spent a summer as a railroad "news butcher," selling newspapers and snacks while crisscrossing six states.

Life with Elias and Flora could not help but seem bland and boring after the romantic life of the railroad. But in the fall, Disney reluctantly joined his family in Chicago and entered McKinley High School.

It was there that he found his first taste of success as a cartoonist when the high school magazine published his

cartoons. Disney had studied the political cartoons in the socialist newspaper his father read, and many of his drawings revolved around the Great War, as World War I was then known.

Like many boys, Walt's imagination was fired by propaganda about the "war to end all wars." Walt's dreams of making the world safe for democracy only grew more grandiose when Roy enlisted in the U.S. Navy. "He used to come down and visit," said Disney, "and gee, he looked swell in that uniform. So I wanted to join him."

Although Elias could not understand his son's fascination with cartooning, Walt studied drawing at the Chicago Institute of Art three nights a week. He also visited the newspaper offices of the editorial cartoonists who were among his instructors. The aspiring cartoonist drank in every detail and absorbed the drawing styles of his editorial heroes into his own technique.

Walt worked for his father, this time washing the glass jars and doing other equally menial chores in the jelly factory. As always, the pay from his father was poor, so when school ended for the summer Walt applied for a job at the post office. Turned down because, at age 16, he was too young, Disney applied his theatrical expertise in the form of a few lines painted on his face. He returned to the same employment window wearing his father's suit, and the "18-year-old" was hired on the spot.

Most of the work was outdoors, collecting and delivering mail from the downtown hotels in a horse-drawn mail wagon. The experienced horse stopped at every point on the mail route with no prompting from Disney.

With spending money in his pocket, Disney enjoyed himself, escorting girls from McKinley High to his favorite entertainments: vaudeville shows and movies. Fascinated with "the flickers" and the technology that produced them, Disney bought his own movie camera.

Mounting it on a tripod, he filmed himself as Charlie Chaplin.

The war was more and more on the young man's mind as the Allies gained the upper hand that summer of 1918. Roy was still in the navy and Walt's older brother Ray had joined the army. Walt would have suited up in a minute, but once again he was too young.

Another 16-year-old post office worker, Russell Maas, told Walt about a Red Cross volunteer unit called the American Ambulance Corps that needed drivers for emergency vehicles in France. Disney and Russell pretended to be brothers and signed up; the age requirement was only 17, and they passed.

There was still the matter of passports, however, and that meant parental signatures. Elias refused to sign; however, Flora, still aching from the flight of three of her sons, preferred to know Walt was in France rather than have him simply disappear one night. She signed the application and forged her husband's name. Walt then took the pen and altered his birth year to read "1900."

But before the boys could be shipped overseas, Disney caught influenza. This was the great Spanish influenza epidemic of 1918; 20 million people were killed worldwide, more than twice the number killed in World War I. A savvy ambulance driver took Disney home even though the boy had been ordered to a hospital; the driver knew that a frightening number of those who went into the hospital did not come out alive. At home, Flora nursed the delirious erstwhile soldier and his little sister, who had also become ill, even after she herself caught the disease.

At last, after weeks of sickness, the fever broke. Disney hurried back to the Ambulance Corps as soon as his weakened muscles would allow him, but it was too late. The rest of the unit, including Russell Maas, had shipped out to France.

On November 11, 1918, the Armistice was signed, and the biggest, bloodiest, most costly war the world had ever known was over. The reaction of Disney and his fellow drivers was disappointment. "We were so darn naive, we didn't know what it meant," admitted Disney in later years. "We just knew that we'd missed out on something."

With the fire of patriotic fever doused and his motivation for serving gone, Disney's thoughts turned back

An old-fashioned political cartoon by Thomas Nast (1840–1902) entitled "The Crowning Insult to Him Who Occupies the President's Chair" shows a lion being crowned as a scapegoat. Disney's original goal as an artist was to become a political cartoonist; he studied the political cartoons in his father's socialist newspapers and drew cartoons for a high school magazine.

to civilian life. One early morning as he lay sleeping in the barracks, the lights suddenly blazed to life. A bunkmate awakened Disney from his sound sleep; 50 men were being shipped out. Disney turned over and went back to sleep; he knew his chance to serve had come and gone. He was wrong. The 50th name called was Walter Elias Disney. The assignment was in France, which seemed to Disney an exotic, far-off land full of enticing adventure. Though the war was over, the Red Cross was still in France for cleanup operations. The food and shelter there were substandard; Disney slept under newspapers and ate pork and beans. On December 5, his friends threw him a surprise birthday party at a local cafe. The guest of honor was stuck with the bill and had to sell his extra pair of shoes to pay it.

Disney was assigned to a motor pool. He drove officers all over Paris, learning the city intimately. Transferred to a canteen at Neufchâteau, Disney drew cartoons for his friends, and he decorated ambulances and even jackets with his drawings. A driver from Georgia asked Disney to decorate German helmets with camouflage. The Georgian then shot holes in the helmets and even attached hair; he then sold these supposedly battleworn artifacts to homebound doughboys, earning a tidy profit for himself and Disney. Walt also earned a reputation as an expert tour guide and drove all types of visitors through the towns of France and Germany.

Back in Paris, Disney met up with Russell Maas. The boys planned on sailing a raft down the Mississippi River after they returned home. Both friends bought German shepherd puppies; Disney named his dog Carey, after one of his favorite editorial cartoonists, Carey Orr. He entrusted Carey to Russell, and the young men arranged to meet again stateside.

When the American Ambulance Corps disbanded in 1919, Disney returned to Chicago. There he found that his dog had died, Russell had lost interest in voyaging down the Mississippi, and Disney's girlfriend had mar-

An American Red Cross vehicle takes Parisian children on an outing in France in 1918. The 16-year-old Walt Disney volunteered for the Red Cross in 1918, serving in the American Ambulance Corps at the conclusion of World War I.

ried someone else. He considered his next move; though still a teenager, Disney felt and acted more mature than his years, and it seemed somehow silly to return to high school. His ever pragmatic father had a job lined up for Disney at the jelly factory for $25 dollars a week. Years later, Disney remembered his response: "I said, 'Dad, I want to be an artist!' And my dad, he just couldn't buy that."

Disney bundled up his drawings and caught the train for Kansas City, where Roy had found work as a teller at the First National Bank after his discharge from the navy in 1919. The two brothers were overjoyed to see each other and swapped stories of their overseas experiences throughout the night.

Walt wasted no time in taking his drawings to the Kansas City newspapers; however, there were no openings for political cartoonists. Like Elias, Roy advised his brother to find a more practical living, but Walt was determined to work as an artist. Finally, Roy heard that a commercial art firm, Pesmen-Rubin, needed an apprentice. The owners, Louis Pesmen and Bill Rubin, liked Disney's drawings and his enthusiasm. In October 1919, they hired him.

Disney's employers were not disappointed. The youthful artist worked quickly and well, finishing assignments that normally took a full day in three hours flat. There the 17-year-old Disney made friends with another young artist just a year older than he was. The son of Dutch immigrants, his name was Ubbe Iwwerks, later shortened to the relatively simple Ub Iwerks. Walt shared with Ub his lettering sample consisting of variations on his name, such as Walter E. Disney, Walter Elias Disney, and Walt Disney. When Walt asked Ub which version he liked best, Ub chose Walt Disney.

But Disney's career as a commercial artist was short-lived. Both he and Ub were laid off after the preholiday rush. The two young artists made a fateful decision: they decided to go into business for themselves. Their first client was Walt Pfeiffer's father, who hired Disney and Iwerks to design a union newsletter. Another client, a former Disney neighbor, gave the young men office space in exchange for design work on a restaurant trade publication.

This venture would prove to be only temporary as well. When Iwerks saw an advertisement for a "first class" artist, Disney and Iwerks agreed that Walt should apply for the job, work part-time, and devote the rest of his time to their fledgling business. Disney was hired by the Kansas City Slide Company. The position, however, was full-time, not part-time. Ub assured Walt that he could manage the business, but Iwerks was not the go-getting salesman that Walt was, and Iwerks-Disney faded into oblivion. Walt angled a job for Ub at the slide company, now renamed the Kansas City Film Ad Company to reflect the company's increased use of drawings that moved.

Disney was intrigued by the one-minute commercials that Kansas City Film Ad produced for projection in movie theaters before the main feature. He liked the idea of cartoons that danced across the big screen. When the *Kansas City Journal* called and offered Walt a position as a political cartoonist, he turned it down. A few short months before, this would have been a dream job. But now his whole life had changed: Walt Disney had seen his future, and it was animation.

4 Walt's Wonderland

WHENEVER HE SAW SOMETHING NEW, especially something technological or mechanical, Walt Disney just had to know how it worked. Once anything was explained to Disney, he grasped it immediately. So when the friendly cameraman at Film Ad showed Disney how the company's cartoons were made—cutout paper figures were moved bit by bit under the camera and photographed one frame at a time—it was just a matter of time before Disney was experimenting with the technique himself.

But Disney was dissatisfied with the crude animation used by Film Ad. He watched the cartoons in the local theater and saw how smoothly Felix the Cat or Mutt and Jeff moved compared to Film Ad's cutout characters. These theatrical cartoons, produced in New York, used drawings, not cutouts. Disney wanted to learn how animation with drawings was done. In the Kansas City Public Library, he found Eadweard Muybridge's classic photographic studies of humans and animals in motion and a basic handbook on animation.

In 1925, Walt Disney, only 23 years old, already had his own film studio in Hollywood.

Disney began following the principles and procedures explained in the books, and the improvement in Film Ad's product was immediately evident. Disney's employers were pleased, and soon Disney and Iwerks were making cartoons with drawn animation for Kansas City Film Ad.

Disney worked tirelessly, improving Film Ad's productions however he could. Bored with the dull copy provided him, he added puns and visual humor, earning the fledgling filmmaker his first intoxicating laughs from a movie theater audience. Borrowing one of Film Ad's animation cameras, Walt set it up in the Disney garage with Roy's help and spent hours every evening experimenting with animation techniques.

Combining his love of editorial cartooning with his newly acquired animating skill, Disney produced a short cartoon decrying the poor condition of Kansas City's streets. Disney added an intriguing touch by having his own hand seem to draw the pictures in the cartoon. After he screened the resulting footage for the manager of the Newman Theater Company, which had a chain of three Kansas City movie theaters, Disney was commissioned to produce one cartoon a week at his asking price, 30 cents a foot. Only later did it hit him: he had figured the 30-cent amount based on expenses without leaving himself a profit.

But it did not matter to Disney. He was making animated films, short and primitive though they were. Working at Film Ad by day, he spent long hours each night producing cartoons in his garage studio. He treated each subject with inventive humor; responding to the perennial problem of silent-picture audience members who read the title cards aloud, Disney portrayed these talkative patrons being dropped through a trapdoor and deposited on the street. Disney dubbed the funny little cartoons Newman Laugh-O-grams.

Disney wanted to emulate the New York animators and asked for sheets of celluloid on which his animation drawings could be traced. The celluloid arrived stained from previous use, and Disney and his helpers had to clean each sheet by hand.

Disney's ambition was to expand beyond the advertising film; he wanted to make cartoons that were pure entertainment. His boss at Kansas City Film Ad was uninterested in any sort of risky expansion. Disney realized that if he was to grow in the animation business he would have to start his own company.

During this time, there were unexpected disruptions in Disney's family. Stolid, responsible Roy was earning good take-home pay and was on the verge of marrying his longtime sweetheart, Edna Francis, when he was stricken with tuberculosis and was sent to a veterans hospital in New Mexico to recuperate in the dry air.

Furthermore, Elias Disney was yet again faced with failure. The jelly factory went bust and he lost everything. He and Flora moved from Chicago to Kansas City, where the family was temporarily reunited. In late 1921, however, Elias, Flora, and Ruth left Kansas City to live with Herb, who had been transferred to Oregon. Tears stung Disney's eyes as he bade them good-bye at the train station. He knew he was alone.

Disney's determination did not desert him, however. He rented a small shop for a studio and began work on the first of a projected series of jazzed-up fairy tales. With the help of three apprentices, Disney labored for six months on the cartoon. Satisfied with the picture, he left the Film Ad Company and, in May 1922, incorporated Laugh-O-gram Films with money from local investors. Just 20 years old, Walt Disney was president of his first company.

Though he spoke with an unpolished midwestern twang and sometimes used the crude language of the outhouse or barracks, Disney could be extremely persuasive, a gift that would serve him well time and again throughout the years. He convinced Iwerks and several other eager young artists to join his fledgling studio. Almost immediately, a distribution deal was set with Pictorial Clubs of Tennessee; they wanted six cartoons, and Disney began production on more of the breezy fairy tales.

Disney bought a live-action camera and used it to earn extra cash for Laugh-O-grams by filming special events for the newsreels and photographing babies for movie-struck parents. He also drove around town filming street scenes, with a sign on his car announcing that the footage could be seen the following night at the Isis theater. Hoping to see themselves on-screen, audiences flocked to the theater, which gave Disney a percentage of the ticket

Walt Disney, wielding a pistol, contributes his acting talents to an early production of his Laugh-O-gram film company. The scene was filmed on a Kansas City rooftop in 1922.

sales. Unfortunately, this surplus money became the company's only source of income, as the completed cartoons were shipped to Pictorial Clubs with no payment sent in return. The Laugh-O-gram distributor, it turned out, was bankrupt.

Iwerks returned to Film Ad; the other animators also left. Disney moved out of his rented room and into the tiny Laugh-O-gram office. The kindly owners of the Greek restaurant downstairs allowed him to eat on credit. Roy sent Walt a blank check, giving him permission to fill it in for any amount up to $30. Walt cashed the check for the full amount.

Finally, a local dentist, Thomas McCrum, asked Disney to produce a film promoting dental hygiene. Disney sheepishly admitted that he was unable to visit the dentist's office to close the deal because he had no shoes. Disney did not have the $1.50 needed to pick up his footwear from the repair shop. Dr. McCrum brought Disney the $1.50 and agreed to pay the much needed sum of $500 for *Tommy Tucker's Tooth*.

Disney cast about for a new project to save Laugh-O-grams. "I was desperately trying to get something that would take hold, catch on," he later remembered. "I was thinking if I had something with a novel twist to it, I might crack the market." Max Fleischer was producing a popular series of shorts, "Out of the Inkwell," in which cartoon characters cavorted in a live-action setting. Disney hit upon the idea of reversing the process and began work on a short called *Alice's Wonderland,* in which a little girl, filmed in live action, enters an animated fantasy world based on the Lewis Carroll book. Disney sent out word to the New York distributors that he had "something new and clever in animated cartoons!"

Unfortunately, with work on *Alice's Wonderland* not quite finished, Disney ran completely out of funds. He later described how he "finally came to a great conclusion. I had missed the boat. I had got in too late. Film cartooning had been going on for all of six or seven years. My only hope lay in live-action movies."

In July 1923, Disney packed up his meager belongings—including the unfinished *Alice's Wonderland*—in a cardboard suitcase and boarded a train bound not East where the animation industry was centered, but West where movies were made in the sun-splashed mecca called Hollywood. Walt moved in with his uncle Robert Disney; Roy was nearby in a veterans' hospital, still recuperating from tuberculosis.

More than 40 years later, Disney vividly recalled his first Hollywood experiences: "For two months I tramped

Walt Disney's first major innovation was placing a live actor in an animated setting in *Alice's Wonderland*. Although the film was never finished, the incomplete footage was impressive enough to land Disney a contract for a series of Alice Comedies that enabled him to start a new studio in Hollywood.

from one studio to another trying to sell myself as a writer, a director, a day laborer—anything to get through those magic gates of big-time show business."

Incredibly, it was cautious Roy's idea that Walt should take up animation again. Despairing of finding work with a major studio, Walt rigged up an animation stand in Uncle Robert's garage. Disney felt the novelty of *Alice's Wonderland* might still give him a step up in the cartoon industry. Disguising his true circumstances, he sent the incomplete footage to distributor Margaret Winkler in New York with the following letter:

> This is to inform you that I am no longer connected with the Laugh-O-gram Films, Inc., of Kansas City, Mo., and that I am establishing a studio in Los Angeles for the purpose of producing the new and novel series of cartoons I have previously written about.
>
> The making of these new cartoons necessitates being located in a production center, that I may engage trained talent for my casts, and be within reach of the right facilities for producing. I am taking with me a select number of my former staff and will in a very short time be producing at regular intervals. . . .

Disney was overjoyed when Winkler wired back, "believe series can be put over . . . will pay fifteen hundred each negative for first six and to show my good faith will pay full amount on each of these six immediately on delivery of negative. . . ."

Without delay Disney caught a bus for the veterans' hospital where Roy was recuperating. Arriving at night, Walt excitedly awakened his brother—and other patients in the ward—with his news. This was Walt's big break in the cartoon business, but he knew he could not do it alone. He needed Roy.

Roy signed himself out of the hospital the next morning. The brothers borrowed $500 from their skeptical uncle Robert and on October 16, 1923, signed a deal with Winkler, thus establishing the first cartoon studio in Hollywood. They named their new company the Disney Brothers Studio. In February 1924, they moved into a small storefront at 4649 Kingswell with "Disney Bros. Studio" painted on the window. "I'll make the name Disney famous around the world," boasted Walt to his father.

Roy used a secondhand camera to film the live action for the Alice Comedies, while Walt slaved over the animation. Realizing he needed an artist who was both fast and good, he again turned to Ub Iwerks, offering a piece of the business to his old partner. "I am glad you made your mind to come out," wrote Disney when Iwerks agreed to leave Kansas City to join the fledgling Disney Studio. "Boy, you will never regret it—this is the place for you—real country to work and play in. . . . I can give you a job as artist-cartoonist . . . with the Disney Productions, most of the work would be cartooning."

Disney felt his own limited draftsmanship held up production. He was a capable draftsman, especially by the standards of the industry at the time. But he wanted only the best talent working with him, and Ub Iwerks definitely fit the bill. From then on, Disney focused on developing stories and gags and on overall production. Never again would he animate or even draw for one of his own cartoons.

The tiny studio produced such titles as *Alice and the Three Bears* and *Alice Cans the Cannibals*. With Iwerks on board, there was a noticeable upswing in quality in the Alice comedies. It was during this period, however, that Disney began to have trouble with his distributor. Margaret Winkler had married and retired; her business was now run by her husband, Charles Mintz, who took a firm hold of the purse strings. Falsely claiming financial difficulty, Mintz began sending Disney only half the promised amount for each short. This decrease, along with the money now set aside for Iwerks's salary, meant less money for the Disney brothers, and less meant hardly any at all. To economize, Walt and Roy shared a single room in a boardinghouse and often split one cafeteria meal between them.

Disney continued to improve both the technical and humorous content of his cartoons, and the animated comedies gained public and critical acclaim. *Motion Picture News,* in reviewing *Alice's Wild West Show,* said that "Walt Disney, the cartoonist, produced a novel combination of an actual cast and cartoons . . . it is highly amusing and wholly entertaining."

The Disney Brothers Studio reached a new financial plateau when Mintz contracted for 18 more Alice pictures at $1,800 per film, plus a share in the profits from rentals paid by theaters. Walt and Roy splurged on new suits, but they put most of the money back into the studio by hiring more animators, some of them former Laugh-O-gram staffers.

One new employee was Lillian Bounds, who had recently come to Hollywood from Idaho. She was an "ink and paint girl," one of the women responsible for tracing the animators' pencil drawings onto sheets of transparent acetate, or cels, and painting the appropriate colors on the reverse side. Walt would sometimes give this young woman a ride home in his newly purchased secondhand car, a Moon roadster, and romance blossomed.

Walt and Roy felt cramped in their small flat. When Walt complained about Roy's cooking once too often, Roy telegraphed Edna Francis. She joined Roy in California, and at last they were married on April 7, 1925. Walt was best man, and Lillian was maid of honor. Three months later, on July 13, 1925, Walt and Lilly were married in Lewiston, Idaho. The ceremony was held in Lillian's brother's house, and the only other member of either family in attendance was Lillian's mother. After the wedding, the couple boarded a train for Seattle, Washington. It was a brief vacation, however, as Walt cut short their honeymoon after a single day in Washington to return to work at the studio.

A week before Walt's wedding, the Disney brothers had bought a lot at 2719 Hyperion Avenue in Los Angeles. The cartoon studio had outgrown its storefront location, and Disney wanted to build a real cartoon studio with room for more artists and expanded production. In early 1926, the Disneys moved into their new space, a pseudo-Spanish stucco building on Hyperion Avenue. The studio changed its name as well as its address; from then on, it would be known as the Walt Disney Studios. Disney figured one name and one personality would make for stronger box office identification. Roy, with little interest in self-promotion, agreed.

At age 24, Disney played the role of director and producer with a passion. Having failed in Kansas City, he was determined to succeed in Hollywood, and his determination bordered on obsession. Disney spent every waking moment refining his productions. In the evenings, Lilly often joined Walt at the studio, dozing on the couch as her husband worked late into the night.

Disney dressed in attire fashionable for young men in the Roaring Twenties. He favored multicolored sweaters, flashy ties, knickers, and a hat worn at a rakish angle. Having grown a mustache on a bet, he kept it, liking the maturity it lent his youthful face.

Disney's staff was equally youthful, and he encouraged his artists to take time out from their demanding work for recreation. A lunchtime baseball game became a daily ritual in a nearby lot. Disney rarely joined in; though a fierce competitor, he never learned to play ball with any certainty.

Disney was churning out one Alice Comedy after another, and the gimmick of the live girl in a cartoon world was running thin. Carl Laemmle, head of Universal Studios, wanted a new cartoon series about a rabbit. Oswald the Lucky Rabbit became Disney's next star.

After a false start with a fat, rather elderly Oswald, Disney came up with a winner: a sleeker, more appealing rabbit. The new, improved Oswald caught on with audiences, and Disney learned that a strong starring personality was crucial to the success of his cartoons. Disney, himself, was far from satisfied with animation's status quo. He wanted to make a difference. "With more money and time, I felt that we could make better pictures and shake ourselves out of the rut."

The Disney product was already beginning to stand out above the competition. Reviewers praised the new Oswald cartoon series: "The animation is good and the clever way in which Disney makes his creations simulate

After losing control of his franchise character, Oswald the Lucky Rabbit, to a ruthless distributor, Disney resuscitated his studio with the help of a mischievous mouse named Mickey and his sweetheart, Minnie.

the gestures and expressions of human beings adds to the enjoyment."

Disney initiated techniques which, to Roy's consternation, reduced or eliminated profits. Going one giant step beyond the flipping of drawings to check the animation's effectiveness, Disney photographed the pencil animation drawings and projected them. He authorized production to continue if the scene worked; if not, it went back to the animator for changes. Over the years, this "pencil test" technique played a key role in Disney's refinement of character animation.

In February 1928, Walt and Lilly traveled to New York to renegotiate with Mintz. The long train journey was a treat for the young couple. Disney was happy with the popularity of Oswald and was confident he could secure more money.

But once in New York, Disney had a rude awakening when Mintz offered even less money than before. Mintz revealed that Disney had no choice: Mintz had surreptitiously signed most of Walt's animators, with the exception of Ub Iwerks and a few others. Disney would have to either accept Mintz's offer—which included giving Mintz half-ownership of his studio—or he would lose his staff. Disney could not even take Oswald to another distributor; according to the fine print of the original contract he had signed with Mintz, Oswald was the property of Universal Pictures.

It was a crushing blow for Disney. Many of his artists had been with him since Kansas City. Now they were deserting him, and the sense of personal betrayal was overwhelming. However, Friz Freleng, one of the defectors to Mintz's outfit, Snappy Comedies, and later a director of Warner Bros. *Looney Tunes* cartoons, claimed that despite Disney's efforts to create a happy family atmosphere, Disney was a "harsh taskmaster, severe and not always reasonable in his criticism." In his opinion,

"The many early defections were the results of his high-strung temperament and his inability to work harmoniously with his men."

Whatever his relationship with his employees had been, Disney now no longer had a staff, and worse, he had no star; Oswald, the successful character he had done so much to create and develop, legally belonged to someone else. Disney vowed to his wife that he would never again work for anybody else.

Sadly, Disney boarded the train to return to the West Coast. There was still hope, if he could only think up a new character—someone who would make people forget all about Oswald the Lucky Rabbit.

5 ✫ A Better Built Mouse

MICKEY MOUSE, Disney later said, "popped out of my mind . . . on a train ride from Manhattan to Hollywood, at a time when the business and fortunes of my brother Roy and myself were at lowest ebb and disaster seemed right around the corner."

In his Laugh-O-gram office in Kansas City, Disney had adopted as a pet a frisky mouse named Mortimer. As he told the story, "Mice gathered in my wastebasket when I worked late at night. I lifted them out and kept them in little cages on my desk. One of them was my particular friend." Disney initially wanted to name his new cartoon character Mortimer, after his old pet, but Lilly objected and suggested Mickey as a less pretentious, more sprightly moniker.

Once Walt was back in California, Ub Iwerks designed the visual appearance of Mickey. The early Mouse looks quite similar to Oswald, whose design in turn was influenced by Felix the Cat. But with Mickey Mouse, Disney and Iwerks hit upon a graphic image with universal appeal. Longtime Disney artist and designer John Hench narrowed it down to Mickey's viewer-friendly

---

Walt Disney poses with Mickey Mouse, the character that saved his studio. Mickey's career was launched in 1928 with the successful short film *Steamboat Willie,* which also introduced sound into animated cartoons.

roundness: "I'm oversimplifying it, but circles have never hurt anybody—they are women's breasts and clouds and other soft forms. Felix the Cat, on the other hand, was full of angles and sharp points."

Mickey may have been poised for stardom, but first he had to reach the screen. Walt and Roy knew that the company had only enough money left to make three cartoons featuring their new character. If none of them sold, they would be out of business before the public ever got a chance to meet Mickey.

Three Oswald cartoons were still due on the old contract, and the departing animators had to work alongside their ex-partners for another month to complete them. To maintain secrecy, Iwerks animated the first Mickey Mouse cartoon, *Plane Crazy* (inspired by the public obsession with aviator Charles Lindbergh, the first person to fly solo across the Atlantic Ocean), behind locked doors. Determined to break Krazy Kat artist Bill Nolan's record of 600 drawings a day, Iwerks singlehandedly drew Mickey's solo flight in a phenomenal two weeks, turning out 700 drawings a day.

Disney produced a second Mickey cartoon, *The Gallopin' Gaucho,* in 1928. Unfortunately, though prospective distributors liked Mickey Mouse, no one would take on the series. Disney had an unproven star and only one more chance to gain a distributor. His funds were quickly draining away.

Meanwhile, a full blown revolution had just broken out in Hollywood—sound. Warner Bros. released *The Jazz Singer* in 1927, and its few scenes with a synchronized soundtrack created a sensation. Some in Hollywood feared the changes sound would bring to the film business; others regarded it as a passing fad. Disney, however, recognized at once that the silent era was over and saw only the creative possibilities in the new technological advancement. "Sound effects and talking pictures are more than a mere novelty," he told Roy. "They are here to stay and in time will develop into a wonderful thing."

Disney daringly conceived the third Mickey Mouse short, *Steamboat Willie,* as a sound cartoon. No one had yet applied sound technology to cartoons with any success, but the potential seemed great, as cartoons could sidestep many of the problems associated with recording live actors at the same time as they were being filmed. Other companies besides Disney's were working to integrate sound into their cartoons as well; even Charles Mintz was trying to add a voice to Disney's old character, Oswald. There was still time, however, to beat out the major studios and launch Mickey Mouse's career with the full benefit of sound.

But would audiences really accept the illusion of speech and song coming from the drawn characters? Disney had to find out. Roy projected a sequence from the incomplete cartoon onto a bedsheet screen through a window, so the clattering of the projector was effectively

Disney cavorts with his staff; from left to right are Disney, Ub Iwerks, Rudolf Ising, and Hugh Harman.

silenced. Disney and several of his artists provided a live soundtrack with harmonicas, whistles, and spittoon drums. Disney recalled, "I visited a lot of five-and-dime stores and bought a bunch of gadgets—night-club noise-makers, cowbells and tin pans. We had washboards on which we could make scrubbing noises. I bought a couple of 'plummer's friends' and some slide whistles and ocarinas [a type of flute]. We played around with those things for a while to work out sound effects; then we began to lay out the score for our sound synchronization."

In Hollywood, sound equipment was monopolized by the major studios, so Disney set out on a quest to find a sound system on the East Coast. He arrived in New York only to find the sound systems too expensive or too inadequate to consider. After attending a screening of Paul Terry's talking cartoon *Dinner Time,* the first to use a new sound system developed by RCA, Disney came away unimpressed. "My God—terrible," he telegraphed Roy, reporting that the system offered "A lot of racket and nothing else."

Finally, Disney met the flamboyant P. A. "Pat" Powers, who had an independent—actually, pirated—sound system called Powers Cinephone. Powers smelled promotional possibilities for his bootleg system and promised to help Disney find a distributor. Disney was sold on the idea and arranged for a recording session. It was a costly disaster. The conductor was unable to follow the action on the screen and his large, expensive orchestra overwhelmed the simple score and screen action.

Disney had no choice but to pay for a second session, financed by the sale of his beloved Moon roadster. This time, however, the soundtrack was recorded Disney's way, and it was faultless. The musicians could now keep in time with the characters' movements by watching a bouncing ball that had been added to the film.

Disney insisted that every time Mickey touched something there be an accompanying sound; for example, when Mickey tapped the teeth of a cud-chewing cow, a xylophone's merry melody matched his every move. Walt's costly perfectionism made the more financially conservative Roy increasingly nervous. Yet Walt remained exuberantly optimistic, writing his brother from New York, "Why should we let a few dollars jeopardize our chances? I think this is Old Man Opportunity rapping at our door. Let's don't let the jingle of a few pennies drown out his knock."

But even with a perfectly synchronized soundtrack, Disney could not interest any of the major distributors in *Steamboat Willie*. Only Harry Reichenbach, operator of Broadway's Colony Theater, was convinced that the new cartoon would be a sensation. He booked *Steamboat Willie* for two weeks in his prestigious movie palace.

Disney attempts to proceed with the serious business of animation while Mickey and Minnie frolic in the background.

Steamboat Willie premiered on November 18, 1928, and it immediately became the talk of the town. The critics raved, describing the cartoon as "an ingenious piece of work with a good deal of fun. It growls, whines and squawks and makes various other sounds that add to its mirthful quality."

Now all the major distributors courted Disney, but to their disbelief, he turned down their seductive offers. The distributors sought to gain control of Mickey Mouse as their own property, but Disney had learned his lesson with the loss of Oswald and insisted on retaining ownership of the character. Again, Powers seemingly came to the rescue by offering to distribute the Disney cartoons himself. Disney, with relief, accepted Power's deal and headed home.

Back on Hyperion Avenue, Roy exploded when he read the contract's fine print; Disney would have to pay Powers $26,000 a year for 10 years to license Cinephone. Walt shrugged; they needed the sound system, and the steep price was, to him, worth every penny.

Production on more Mickey Mouse sound shorts began in earnest; the next year and a half saw 31 new sound cartoons. While in New York, Disney recruited several top animators, but Iwerks remained his star cartoonist. "The New York animators take off their hats to [Ub's] animation and all of them know who we are," Disney proudly said.

Mickey Mouse became more popular with each new cartoon, soon overtaking not only Felix the Cat and Oswald, but even live-action stars like Buster Keaton, Harold Lloyd, Al Jolson, and even Charlie Chaplin in popularity. Audiences relished Disney's creative use of sound, the lively animation, and especially the happy-go-lucky personality of the brightly smiling Mouse. "Mickey was the first cartoon character to stress personality," Disney later observed. "I thought of him from the first as a distinct individual—not just a cartoon type or a symbol going through a comedy routine."

As pleased as he was with Mickey, Disney knew from his experience with the Alice Comedies that producing one cartoon after another with the same character was a creative drain. "By nature I'm an experimenter," was how Disney put it later. "So, with the success of Mickey, I was determined to diversify. I had another idea which was plaguing my brain—a series without a central character . . . which would give me the latitude to develop the animated cartoon medium." He decided to call the series *Silly Symphony* cartoons.

The first of the *Silly Symphony* cartoons, *The Skeleton Dance,* was inspired by French composer Camille Saint-Saëns's *Danse Macabre* and was animated almost entirely by Ub Iwerks. Disney began to see Iwerks's prodigious output as a waste of his top animator's talents. Disney did not want Iwerks to make every drawing himself; that was what assistants were for. Iwerks refused to do it Disney's way. It was not the first time Iwerks resented taking orders from his ex-partner.

Powers was not interested in the macabre *Skeleton Dance* with its bony chorus line performing an eerie ballet. He was well aware that the lucrative contract he had with Disney would not apply to the new series. But Disney bypassed his distributor and booked the *Silly Symphony* cartoon into two theaters himself. Though audiences enjoyed the creepy cartoon and its novel mix of action and music, theater owners were wary of the new cartoons, so Disney agreed to release them under the heading, MICKEY MOUSE PRESENTS A WALT DISNEY SILLY SYMPHONY.

Despite the box office appeal of Mickey's name, money was not coming in at a rate commensurate with the Mouse's huge popularity. Roy was convinced that Powers was cheating the Disneys and hired an independent auditor, who discovered a discrepancy between Powers's figures and the actual box office receipts. Walt hired a lawyer, Gunther Lessing, and went to New York to confront the unscrupulous distributor. Instead of showing Disney the books, Powers offered to take over the studio and pay Walt a salary to run it. Of course, Disney was not about to give control of his studio to anyone. But the slick distributor thought he had the upper hand: he told Disney that he had signed Ub Iwerks away to start his own studio.

Disney was shocked at this double betrayal. He had trusted Powers; as for Iwerks, Ub had been his first partner and even now was part owner of the Disney Studio. Powers, of course, did not want Iwerks—he wanted leverage over Disney to get Mickey Mouse. His maneuver was futile; Disney wanted nothing more to do with either of them. He told Powers he could have the animator.

Ub's son, Dave Iwerks, later explained to Disney biographer Marc Eliot, "Ub and Walt were both very hardheaded, and because of that any differences between them became major. My father felt overworked and underappreciated at Disney. He'd begun as a partner and was now an employee. When Powers gave Ub the chance to start his own studio, he jumped at it. And why shouldn't he have?"

The Disneys bought out Iwerks's share of the company for $3,000. From a purely financial standpoint, Iwerks's decision would not turn out to be a wise one, as the shares today would have been worth around one-half billion dollars. Disney broke off with Powers, though Roy had to pay off the distributor to the tune of $100,000—a vast sum, but the Disneys considered the amount worth it to be out of his grasp. Iwerks opened his own studio and created cartoons starring Flip the Frog, with scant success.

Disney's career, on the other hand, continued to sky-rocket. Theaters billed his cartoons above the alleged feature attraction, and "What—no Mickey Mouse?" became a countrywide catchphrase for disappointment. Mickey's beaming likeness appeared on hundreds of pieces of merchandise from cards to drinking glasses and toothbrushes. Mickey even rescued at least two companies—Ingersoll watches and Lionel trains—from bankruptcy through sales of Mickey Mouse merchandise.

Disney continued to push his growing staff of animators to make each cartoon better than the previous one. Disney drove himself hardest of all, and his workaholic habits began to catch up with him. He was unable to sleep, had crying jags, and his mind suddenly went blank during story meetings. Adding to his troubled state were two miscarriages suffered by Lilly. Disney later said of this period, "I guess I was working too hard and worrying too much. . . . I had a nervous breakdown."

Disney's doctor recommended a vacation, and Walt and Lilly, taking their first non-business trip since their honeymoon, took a long "gypsy jaunt" around the country, ending with a 5,000-mile cruise from Cuba to Los Angeles. Back home, Disney took his doctor's advice to introduce exercise into his regular routine. He and Lilly both took up horseback riding.

The Hyperion studio expanded almost as fast as Mickey's popularity soared. New buildings were added in 1931, including a soundstage. Here, Disney himself recorded Mickey's voice, a friendly but hesitant falsetto that cracked and often dropped down into the lower register, perhaps because of Disney's heavy smoking. Disney continued to provide Mickey's voice until the mid-1940s, when he became too busy. No one else has ever been able to breathe the rich midwestern warmth into Mickey's voice that Walt Disney brought to the part.

Disney also exercised his performing talents by acting out the characters and routines during story meetings. Disney's artists were in awe of his acting abilities; they often said they wished that they could animate an action as well as Walt had performed it. One admiringly called Walt's acting "as good as anything Chaplin had ever done."

Always seeking to improve the quality of his films, Disney continued to incorporate new techniques in his filmmaking. The process of animated storytelling was considerably improved with the Disney innovation of the storyboard. Story artists pinned individual drawings of the action to a large bulletin board, comic strip fashion. As the story evolved, the drawings were moved, redone, or tossed out. The storyboard technique was soon adopted as the industry standard, and today it is also used in advertising and live-action filmmaking.

Another important innovation was color. In 1932, Technicolor introduced the first color process that could reproduce the full spectrum. Disney saw a test reel and exclaimed, "At last! We can show a rainbow on the screen." Roy was not as excited as his brother: color was an added expense, and the Disneys had just signed a profitable distribution deal with United Artists. There would be no extra money for the added expense of color.

Disney believed color would get his cartoons longer and better theater bookings. "I had a picture in work called *Flowers and Trees*," Disney later recalled. "I'd

Disney's high-strung temperament and obsessive work habits occasionally overwhelmed him. He is shown here during a much needed vacation in Cuba in 1931.

finished about half of it in black and white. I just felt that this color would do so much for the cartoon media that it was worth doing the picture over."

Flowers and Trees, complete with a Technicolor rainbow, opened to great acclaim and was the first cartoon to win an Academy Award. Disney had the foresight to secure an exclusive two-year deal for cartoons with Technicolor (freezing out Iwerks's company, which had planned a similar venture), and from then on, Disney made all his *Silly Symphony* cartoons in color. Until this time, the *Silly Symphony* cartoons had been overshad-

Walt Disney and his wife, Lillian, display Disney's first Oscar at the 1932 Academy Awards banquet.

owed by Mickey Mouse, but now Disney's Technicolor cartoons were in demand.

Disney's pursuit of the highest possible technical standards was only part of the reason for his cartoons' appeal. Giving his creatures personalities was Disney's constant ambition for character animation. When Disney began outlining plans for a new *Silly Symphony* entitled *Three Little Pigs,* he wrote, "These little pig characters look as if they would work up very cute and we should be able to develop quite a bit of personality in them."

Three Little Pigs surpassed even Walt's expectations. The pigs, though identical in appearance, had distinct personalities defined by movement. "At last we have achieved true personality in a whole picture!" Walt excitedly told Roy. *Three Little Pigs* was a smash hit; movie patrons lined up to see the seven-minute short. The Pigs' bouncy theme, "Who's Afraid of the Big Bad Wolf?" played from every radio, the first hit song to spring from a cartoon. *Three Little Pigs* won Disney another Academy Award, and the *Silly Symphony* cartoons dominated the Oscars for the rest of the decade. When United Artists demanded, "Send us more pigs!" Disney reluctantly obliged, producing several more *Silly Symphony* cartoons about the Little Pigs, none of which were particularly successful. Thereafter Disney was fond of saying, "You can't top pigs with pigs."

The year 1933 ended on a high note for Disney—on December 18, he became a father when Diane Marie was born. Walt and Lillian had longed to be parents, and Lillian's miscarriages had been devastating losses. So it was with special pleasure that the young couple, who had just moved into a new Tudor-style house, welcomed a baby daughter into the family.

6 ★ Forging an Art Form

THE GREAT DEPRESSION of the 1930s put millions of people out of work, but ironically it provided a boon for the Disney Studio. People sought relief and escapism in the cool darkness of the movie palaces. Mickey Mouse in particular was a shining symbol of optimism in trying times. "Who's Afraid of the Big Bad Wolf?" became a battle hymn for the many citizens who faced a very big, extremely bad wolf at their own doors.

The depression also meant a dearth of jobs for many graduates of art schools. Among the few employers hiring artists in those economically grim days was Walt Disney. Many finely trained artists found their way to Hyperion Avenue, especially once Disney began his hiring drive in the mid-1930s.

But Disney wanted all his artists trained *his* way. "We needed specialized training," Disney later explained. "It was something you couldn't quite get in schools. So I made a deal with some of the [art school] teachers to come out and work with me. To sit with me by day and know my problems." Chief among these was Don Graham from the Chouinard School of Art in Los

---

The immense popularity of Mickey Mouse made Walt Disney a sought-after figure in Hollywood society in the 1930s. He was invited to join two of Hollywood's most exclusive polo clubs and began playing regularly with stars such as Will Rogers, Spencer Tracy, and Leslie Howard (left).

Angeles. Beginning in 1932, Graham taught the Disney Art Class twice a week, exploring movement and life drawing as related to animation.

Disney required rough sketches rather than finished drawings from his artists. Animator Norm Ferguson was Disney's model for this rough-hewn animation that emphasized the entire action being portrayed instead of the individual drawings themselves. To get that "rough quality of Fergy's" into their animation was especially hard for the formally trained artists. But it was this rough approach that led to life and personality, characteristics essential to Disney's evolving vision of animation's potential.

Disney was a man of many moods, some of them dark and difficult. His artists would say they used to call down to the studio gate and see which Walt had come in that day. "I think he was deliberately a different person to different people," said Marc Davis, one of Disney's best animators and designers. "He read something in you and behaved accordingly toward you. I'm sure he behaved differently to me than he did to other people; I think I knew a different Walt than . . . most of the others."

Disney was a demanding if inspiring leader; in his drive to polish the work that came out under his name, he sometimes did not stop to consider the feelings or the egos of his associates, some of whom resented that their collective efforts were often portrayed as the product of Walt Disney's individual genius. Through the years, those who worked with the volatile Disney learned not to take his temper or heated remarks personally.

Technicolor finally came to Mickey Mouse with *The Band Concert* (1935), one of the best shorts produced by the studio. The cartoon costarred a new Disney character, Donald Duck, who was created when Walt heard voice artist Clarence "Ducky" Nash's squawky recital of "Mary Had a Little Lamb." "That's our talking duck!" Disney said. Within a year, the hot-tempered Donald was a serious challenger to Mickey's popularity.

Donald Duck premiered in the 1934 *Silly Symphony*, *The Wise Little Hen*, one of a series of adaptations of fables or fairy tales. Cartoon by cartoon, Disney and his story department were honing their storytelling skills, inspired by the consummate performances of Walt himself.

Disney's greatest performance was on a late evening, sometime in 1934, when he gathered some of his artists in a darkened soundstage. With only a single bulb as his spotlight, Disney told the story of *Snow White and the Seven Dwarfs*. Walt held his staff spellbound as he acted out every part—the evil Queen, the innocent Snow White, and the comical dwarfs. When he finished, he turned to his staff, many of whom had tears in their eyes. "That's going to be our first feature," he proclaimed.

Disney examines a musical score in 1939. Although he had previously not been a fan of classical music, Disney fell in love with symphonic music while making *Fantasia*, an elaborate series of animated images inspired by famous pieces of classical music.

An animated feature film was a revolutionary concept. Though a couple of lengthy animated films had been produced in Europe, it seemed inconceivable for an animated cartoon of any length to seriously compete with live-action films. Roy was completely against the idea. It seemed to him that every time the studio started to get a little bit ahead, Walt found a way to get them back in the red. Walt ignored his brother; he would make his feature, no matter what. Disney gathered a small unit of artists to develop what he called the "feature Symphony."

As he slaved over *Snow White* and the short cartoons in 1935, Disney began to lose his usual laserlike concentration. Roy feared another breakdown, and he suggested to Walt that they take their wives on a 10th wedding anniversary trip to Europe. To Roy's relief, Walt agreed. Perhaps Roy even hoped Walt would forget about his foolish notion of making a feature. But, on the contrary, Walt discovered a Parisian theater that showed six Disney cartoons in a row as its main attraction. Disney returned home more convinced than ever that the feature was feasible.

Disney had his own reasons for choosing the *Snow White* story. "It's a [silent movie] I remember as a kid," he said. "I saw it in Kansas City one time when I was a newsboy. They had a big show for all the newsboys. . . . It was probably one of the first big feature pictures I'd ever seen." Disney also recognized that the story was one he and his artists could really sink their teeth into. "I thought it was a perfect story. I had the heavy, I had the prince and the girl, the romance. I had the sympathetic dwarfs."

From the start, Disney knew that the Seven Dwarfs, only unnamed, characterless figures in the original Grimm's fairy tale, would be crucial to *Snow White*'s success. In *Three Little Pigs,* three distinctive personalities

The multiplane camera developed by the Disney studio allowed Disney animators to create an impression of depth and perspective by photographing several layers of drawings, each of which could be moved independently.

had been achieved; now the number was seven, the Dwarfs were more complex than the pigs, and their characters had to be maintained for the length of a feature. "I wanted no doubt about the personalities," Disney said, "so I picked a name to fit the personality." Thus, Happy would be unmistakably happy, Bashful would be bashful, and so on. But that was only the start; Disney and his artists spent hours discussing and dissecting the Dwarfs—how they moved, talked, interacted, even how they stood or used their hands.

Even more challenging than the Dwarfs was the film's leading lady. Only the broadest of human caricatures had been animated up until that time, and now Disney was asking his staff to create a convincing, engaging, lovely young woman.

The *Silly Symphony* cartoons were the testing ground for new techniques, and Disney assigned Ham Luske to animate a lifelike woman for *The Goddess of Spring*. Luske was disappointed in his Persephone, who ended up with rubbery limbs and a face like a mask. Disney was not discouraged; he and his team learned from the experiment. Disney appointed Luske supervising animator of Snow White.

Meanwhile, the film industry at large thought the idea of making a feature cartoon ludicrous; the *Snow White* project was commonly called "Disney's Folly." But Disney's vision extended beyond what anyone else even imagined the project to be. He had his technicians develop a so-called multiplane camera, an animation camera pointing down through levels of artwork, any of which could be moved toward or away from the camera. The effect was an illusion of depth, overcoming what Disney saw as the limitations of the flat, two-dimensional backgrounds. (Some years earlier, Ub Iwerks had built at his own studio a less versatile prototype out of parts from an old Chevy.)

Disney tested the multiplane camera in *The Old Mill* (1937), a *Silly Symphony* cartoon he described as "just a poetic thing, nothing but music." The intricate multiplane shots achieved mood and depth and proved the specialized camera to be worth the effort and expense. "It was always my ambition to own a swell camera," Disney enthused in an interview with *Time* magazine, "and now, godamm it, I got one."

Disney also filmed live action as reference for the artists; this film was not traced, as is sometimes reported; rather, the animators used the live footage only as a guide. This approach helped Disney and his artists finally achieve a graceful, convincing Snow White. The animated acting achieved by Ham Luske and his fellow animators was equal to much of the best live-action film acting of the day.

Meanwhile, Disney continued to refine the Dwarfs. Early visualizations resemble gnarled elves or gnomes, lacking the warmth and appeal Disney was looking for. His constant directive was to make the Dwarfs "more cute." Eventually the personalities of the Dwarfs were set. There was Doc, the befuddled leader, and Happy, Bashful, Sleepy, Sneezy, and Grumpy. Disney decided to name the seventh Dwarf Dopey, even though some feared the name might be seen as implying drug abuse.

Disney put two of his top animators, Vladimir "Bill" Tytla and Fred Moore, in charge of the Dwarfs. Moore's drawing had charm and grace, and he refined the design of the Dwarfs to Disney's satisfaction. Tytla's vigorous animation firmly established all the Dwarfs' characters through their actions; his animation of Grumpy made the misogynist Dwarf the most complex character in the film, as his attitude toward Snow White changes gradually from dislike to love.

Only Dopey refused to come to life. A voice still had not been found, and his features were not yet satisfactory. Fred Moore finally achieved a more childlike Dopey by infusing much of his own innocent mischief and charm into the Dwarf's design. As for Dopey's voice, Disney decided the Dwarf would not speak at all. The last Dwarf to be perfected, Dopey became an audience favorite.

Hours each day, often including evenings and weekends, were spent on *Snow White*. Disney felt Snow White looked too pale so his painters hand-applied rouge on each individual image of the princess. Animator Frank Thomas drew Dopey taking a little hitch step to catch up with the other Dwarfs; Disney liked it so much that he ordered all animation of Dopey redone to include the hitch step.

Costs mounted alarmingly and Roy continued his opposition to the risky venture. At one screening of the partly finished feature, written responses included the anonymous note "Stick to shorts." Disney was greatly upset by this vote of no-confidence but never discovered who was responsible for it. Some thought it was Roy.

Lilly, too, was deeply concerned over the alarming amount of money being spent on the feature, although she loved *Snow White* itself. Disney's original budget of $500,000 was woefully inadequate. It became apparent that unless the bank loaned Disney more money, the feature would never be finished. With the film a jumble of sketches, storyboards, pencil tests, and several completed scenes, Roy told Walt that they needed a quarter of a million dollars to complete *Snow White*.

The Disney staffers labor in the animation studio. A tireless perfectionist, Disney often made his artists redo a scene until he was completely satisfied with it.

Walt later remembered Roy's exact, chilling words:

"You've got to show the bankers what's been completed on 'Snow White' as collateral." I had always objected to

letting any outsider see an incompleted picture. . . . But Roy went ahead with the arrangements.

However, on the appointed day, my big brother had found something to do elsewhere. I had to sit alone with Joe Rosenberg of the Bank of America and try to sell him a quarter of a million dollars worth of faith. He showed not the slightest reaction to what he viewed. After the lights came on, he walked out of the projection room, remarked that it was a nice day—and yawned!—He was still deadpan as I conducted him to his car. Then he turned to me and said—"Walt, that picture will make a pot full of money."

In a mad rush of concentrated work—most of the actual animation took place in the last year of production—*Snow White* was completed just days before the Christmas 1937 deadline. As the banker predicted, *Snow White and the Seven Dwarfs* smashed box office records, earning an astounding $8 million at a time when the average ticket price was 25 cents for adults and 10 cents for children. Critics were laudatory, calling it "one of the ten best films of the year" and "one of the few great masterpieces of the screen."

Disney basked in the adulation. "Disney's Folly" had become the most popular movie ever made. Naturally, there was a call for "more Dwarfs." But Disney, as usual, was already looking to the future.

Shirley Temple presents Disney with a special Academy Award bearing one large and seven small Oscars awarded for the groundbreaking animated feature film *Snow White and the Seven Dwarfs.*

CALSHIP'S
447th.
U·S·M·C·
SHIP

7 ⋆ Dark Days

THE ACADEMY OF MOTION PICTURE Arts and Sciences honored Walt Disney for producing *Snow White and the Seven Dwarfs* with a special Academy Award, made up of one standard size and seven miniature Oscars. In thanking the Academy for the honor, Disney told the audience of movie stars, executives, and technicians, who all sat in rapt attention for a full 25 minutes, the story of his next animated feature.

There was more in Disney's life to celebrate than his great professional success. He and Lilly adopted a baby girl, Sharon Mae, in January 1937. Another miscarriage had dashed their hopes of ever having another baby, but the Disneys were overjoyed with the addition to their family—although for most of 1937 Walt was rarely at home due to the demands of making *Snow White*, often sleeping instead on a couch in the studio. Later, with the profits he had earned from *Snow White*'s seemingly bottomless diamond mine, Walt was able to build his family a new home surrounded by a garden complete with a waterfall.

Walt Disney and his daughter Diane stand by as Walt's wife, Lillian, christens the SS *Rice Victory*, a 10,500-ton World War II warship, with a bottle of champagne on June 16, 1945.

The Disneys rang in the New Year of 1938 with a family celebration of Elias and Flora's 50th wedding anniversary. It was an especially joyous occasion because Walt and Roy had finally convinced their parents to join them in California. Elias and Flora had been working as hard as ever running a boardinghouse in Oregon, and now the Disney brothers were delighted that their mother and father would be nearby to share in the bounty of the studio's success. Elias and Flora moved into a house in North Hollywood, purchased for them by Walt and Roy.

The overwhelming worldwide success of *Snow White and the Seven Dwarfs* made clear that features were the future for Disney. The Mickey Mouse and Donald Duck

Walt clowns with his brother, Roy, in Honolulu, Hawaii, in November 1939.

cartoons would continue, but the emphasis would now be on feature films to compete on an equal footing with the product of the other Hollywood entertainment factories. Disney planned on releasing one feature per year, with three features in production at any given time. For that kind of output, Disney needed to leave the overflowing Hyperion Avenue facility for a custom-built studio, designed for the optimum production of animated features on a 51-acre site along Buena Vista Street in Burbank.

After all that he and his artists had learned while working on *Snow White,* Disney hoped that the production of his second feature would run much smoother and faster. But *Pinocchio* had its own set of unique challenges. Carlo Collodi's original story of a wooden puppet who comes to life was an imaginative, rambling tale that required extensive revision and compression to be translated to film. Furthermore, Pinocchio, a disobedient delinquent in the original, was not exactly the typical Disney hero. Disney scrapped six months worth of work and went back to the drawing board.

Then, without warning, Disney was dealt a devastating blow. Early one morning in November 1938, a faulty furnace leaked deadly fumes into his parents' house. Elias was overcome by the poisonous gas, but the housekeeper and a neighbor managed to pull him outside in time. For Flora it was too late, and she died of asphyxiation. Both Walt and Roy were shattered; they felt responsible for the tragedy caused by the house they had bought. For the rest of his life, Walt could not bear to even mention his mother's death.

Disney plunged himself into his work with an even greater intensity. Animator Milt Kahl redesigned Pinocchio as a cute little boy; the puppet was transformed into an innocent who did not know the difference between right and wrong. The problem of a passive hero was solved with the addition of Jiminy Cricket as Pinocchio's conscience. Disney assigned Ward Kimball to design this new character, but Walt rejected the first cricketlike designs. Kimball finally modified the insect into something like a cute little bald man.

Disney set out to top himself with *Pinocchio,* and he succeeded. Superb character animation, extensive use of the multiplane camera, painstakingly detailed backgrounds, and spectacular effects made *Pinocchio* a rich visual and emotional experience. Unfortunately, the beginning of World War II in Europe shortly before *Pinocchio*'s release in February 1940 made fantasy seem out of fashion; many foreign markets, responsible for much of Disney's profit margin, were closed because of the European war. Consequently, *Pinocchio* did not earn back its cost of $2.5 million at the box office.

Disney's next feature, *Fantasia,* started as a sort of deluxe *Silly Symphony* cartoon starring Mickey Mouse in a visual interpretation of French composer Paul Dukas's *The Sorcerer's Apprentice.* Walt gained a collaborator in Leopold Stokowski, the famed conductor of the Philadelphia Orchestra known for his dramatic style and wild hair. The conductor encountered Disney at a restaurant, and when Walt told him of the *Sorcerer's Apprentice* project, Stokowski offered to conduct the Dukas piece.

Disney said *The Sorcerer's Apprentice* would be made up entirely of "pantomime and descriptive music." As Disney and Stokowski worked on this concept, it blossomed into an idea for an entire feature consisting of animated musical pieces. Despite the experimental nature of this "Concert Feature," Roy gave it the go-ahead; the production costs for *The Sorcerer's Apprentice* were $125,000, and it would have very little chance of making money if it was shown alone as a short.

For the rest of *Fantasia,* Disney and Stokowski carefully selected compositions that would inspire the artists

to create visuals as potent as the music's aural sensations. Inspired by the music of Beethoven, Tchaikovsky, Stravinsky, and other great composers, Disney and his staff came up with a dizzying variety of virtuoso animated pieces, from relatively traditional Disney material such as dancing hippos and alligators, to special effects extravaganzas picturing the creation of the world, to the truly revolutionary abstract images accompanying Bach's *Toccata and Fugue.*

Disney had never been much of a classical music fan, but now he became fascinated with its emotional, soulful power, especially as experienced at a live performance.

Disney confers with Deems Taylor (center), the narrator of *Fantasia,* and Leopold Stokowski (right), the Philadelphia Symphony Orchestra conductor featured in the film. The film's sound track was recorded in Fantasound, which recreated the sound of a live concert by playing 7 tracks of music over 30 speakers spread throughout the theater.

Though he sometimes fell asleep at concerts, Disney was thrilled by the full sound he experienced in the concert hall. He set his sound department to work on a system of sound reproduction that would create the illusion of a live orchestral performance. The resulting process, dubbed Fantasound by Disney, has been called a precursor of stereo. But it was actually much more. In its use of 7 different tracks (as opposed to 2 in stereo) and 30 speakers to channel the sound to different points in the theater, Fantasound predated such contemporary systems as Dolby and THX by decades.

Fantasia was unveiled on November 13, 1940, nearly 12 years to the day after the premiere of *Steamboat Willie* in the same theater. Disney must have been aware, as he watched the kaleidoscope of images and heard the sound swirl around him, how far animation had come in those few short years, which had seen a quantum leap of quality due to his dedication, drive, and all-consuming perfectionism.

Though reviewers of *Fantasia* could not fault Disney for his bold experimentation—many proclaimed it a revolutionary masterpiece—there was also criticism. Some found it pretentious, and many music critics branded it objectionable. Among the reviewers' comments on *Fantasia* were the most negative Disney had ever received.

Throughout the 1930s, Disney's charming cartoons had been embraced by critics and the intelligentsia for their ingenious comedy and characterizations. But now Disney was seen as trespassing on the sacred ground of high art, and as calculatingly promoting himself as a great artist. Disney was indeed stretching the boundaries of an art form he had all but invented. Many of his former champions resented the direction he was headed and wanted to see Disney stick to his old, familiar style. But, as Disney's productions in general and *Fantasia* in particular made clear, that was something Disney would not do.

The motion picture company RKO, which had gained fame from its Fred Astaire and Ginger Rogers musicals and Katharine Hepburn and Cary Grant comedies, was baffled by Disney's "highbrow" cartoon and gladly allowed Disney to release *Fantasia* himself. According to Disney's own unique plans, *Fantasia* would play only in first-run theaters especially equipped with the entire Fantasound system, and tickets would be sold on a reserved-seat basis, just as at a live concert.

But for once, Disney was not to have his way. The results were disastrous. Only 12 Fantasound units had been built—at $30,000 apiece—when the government, citing national defense priorities, halted production of the sound equipment. Disney's plans to open *Fantasia* in 76 theaters nationwide had to be abandoned.

Disney's backers pressured him to put *Fantasia* into general release to generate as much revenue as possible. RKO insisted that the film was too long and had to be cut. "You can get anybody you want to edit it," Disney responded. "I can't do it." Released with almost an hour missing and on a double bill with a Western, this "radically different type of entertainment," as Disney described *Fantasia,* failed to attract an audience.

The year 1940 saw the move to the Burbank studio completed. Disney had involved himself with every detail of the new plant's design, especially of the animation building. Modern air conditioning, restful color schemes, northern light, and state-of-the-art equipment made it an animators' paradise.

By 1942, the approximate date of this picture, the facilities of the Disney studio in Burbank, California, had become a vast campus.

Elias Disney had never been the same after Flora's death, and the Disney brothers had asked their father to watch over the new studio's carpentry; he puttered around the new studio construction site, pounding in a nail here and there. One day he asked Walt how he expected to support such a big place with cartoons. Disney relieved his father's worries by telling him if the studio failed it could be converted into a hospital.

But Elias's worries were not unfounded. Walt Disney Productions was sinking fast in financially choppy waters. Taking a desperate measure to save their foundering studio, Walt and Roy went public, offering stock for sale. The decision to let others buy into their family company was difficult for both brothers. It was especially difficult for Walt, who did not want outsiders interfering with his creative decisions.

To Walt Disney, the studio was his passion, and his staff was family. Disney had always tried to have a close working relationship with everyone, even the paymaster and the custodial staff, but now, with more than 1,000 employees working at the studio, that was impossible. As for the employees, many, not surprisingly, thought of the studio only as a place to work and thought of Disney not as a father figure but as a figurehead. There was also dissatisfaction with salaries and the isolation of one department from another, an unfortunate side effect of the comfortable but compartmentalized new plant.

Union organizers tried to force Disney to allow his workers to organize, but he refused. He saw a union as unnecessary, paternalistically believing that he provided everything they needed. Not all of his employees enjoyed Walt's attempts at acting fatherly, however. Even when his actions were well intentioned, they could sometimes be an imposition, as he expected to exert a great deal of control over his employees' lives. For example, when Walt's good friend, the movie star Spencer Tracy, taught

Walt to play polo, Disney was thrilled by the game. Wishing to share his pleasure with his animators, he ordered mandatory riding lessons every Sunday in a nearby park, apparently oblivious that many would have preferred to spend their one day off per week as they chose.

In February 1941, the studio's economic troubles and rumors of a strike prompted Disney to address the entire studio. He outlined the studio's history, the sacrifices that he and Roy had made, the hopes he had for animation, and his desire to be just one of the working stiffs. Never before and never again would Walt pour out his heart to his employees. It was a typically moving Disney performance, but he failed to appreciate the anger and resentment of his staff, who were still forbidden to unionize.

Walt's public position was that he would gladly accept a union if it was voted for by the majority of the entire staff. This bargaining point was not acceptable to the animators, who legally had the right to join a union on their own, having marshalled the necessary pledge cards. To them, Walt's position seemed merely an attempt to use his influence with the all-female inkers to defeat the all-male animators.

In May 1941, much to his surprise, Disney found a picket line around the studio. For Walt, it was an emotional matter. As before, Disney was shocked that people he considered family would "betray" him. Ironically, *The Reluctant Dragon,* which in the studio's first use of live action portrayed the Disney Studio as a happy, familylike organization, was released during the strike.

The strike dragged on for months. Disney was unwilling to compromise, often making statements in anger that made him look bad. One of his main targets was animator Arthur Babbitt, who had originally been picked to lead Disney's in-house union before opting for the

Disney auditions his female employees for acting roles. The highly publicized audition was seen as a threat by Disney against his striking animators to shift away from animation toward more films with live actors.

independent Cartoonists Guild. Babbitt later discussed the strike with Marc Eliot, author of the highly critical 1993 biography *Walt Disney: Hollywood's Dark Prince.* (The book—excerpts of which were sold to the *National Enquirer*—contained some new information, including the allegation that Disney had given information to the F.B.I., but it also contained "more than 150 glaring factual errors," according to Lillian Disney and Diane Disney Miller.) Babbitt told Eliot how, in a direct violation of labor-relation laws, Disney fired Babbitt and had him escorted off the lot by two police officers. Babbitt appealed his firing, and on the day of his appointment with the labor board he was arrested for allegedly carrying a concealed weapon. "I was taken to the Burbank jail, and of course it was just a coincidence that the chief of police of Burbank was the brother-in-law of Disney's in-house chief of security. I was not allowed to make any phone calls."

Babbitt said that he would have missed the labor board appointment but for a sympathetic studio vice-president who had it postponed. Babbitt won the hearing, and Disney was ordered to give him back his job. It was not the last time Babbitt would be fired illegally. Disney continued to oppose Babbitt's reinstatement, despite numerous rulings, until 1946, when the Supreme Court quashed Disney's final appeal and awarded Babbitt a large settlement. Nevertheless, references to Babbitt were banned in all public relations documents at the time, although he had been responsible for some of Disney's most critically acclaimed passages, including the dancing mushroom sequence in *Fantasia.*

The strike was finally settled when, at the urging of his brother Roy, Walt left the country on a goodwill tour of South America. The U.S. government offered Disney $100,000 to produce films there if he would agree to lend his reputation to the effort to combat the growing influence of Nazi Germany in South America.

Disney accepted, and beginning in August 1941, he toured Brazil, Argentina, and Chile with a handpicked group of artists. The popularity of Disney's productions was evident in the adoring crowds that mobbed Walt and his entourage wherever they went. Disney and his artists collected material for cartoons based on the culture and locales of South America, including *The Three Caballeros,* a surreal, wildly imaginative feature film in which Donald Duck chases several women played by live actresses. Sadly, the trip caused Disney to miss the funeral of his father, who died while Walt was away.

When Disney returned to Hollywood, the strike had been settled with government arbitration. Time clocks were installed, and Disney removed many of the niceties, including the soda fountain and the gym, that he had built into his animators' paradise. The "Mouse Factory" was now just that.

Although the popularity of Disney films would only grow, the pre-strike era has been called the Disney studio's Golden Age. The costly failures of *Fantasia* and *Pinocchio,* and most especially the bitter strike, changed forever Walt Disney's attitude toward animation. He was blunt: "The spirit that played such an important part in the building of the cartoon medium had been destroyed." Also missing from future Disney projects were many talented animators who had supported the strike and had resigned or been forced out in a wave of layoffs.

How strongly Walt Disney continued to feel about the strike would be revealed six years later in his testimony to the House Un-American Activities Committee (HUAC) on October 24, 1947. HUAC was a congressional committee formed in 1938 to investigate alleged Communists whose activities were considered a threat to American democracy. Referring to the strikers, Disney testified, "I definitely feel it was a Communist group trying to take over my artists and they did take them over." When asked to name names, Disney fingered labor organizer Herbert Sorrell, the leader of the strike. The only evidence offered in support of his claim was, "I believed at the time that Mr. Sorrell was a Communist because of all the things that I had heard and having seen his name appearing on a number of Commie front things." Sorrell was fired as president of the Congress of Studio Unions, and a year later he died of a heart attack.

The 1940s and 1950s would witness one of the darkest chapters in American history, known as the McCarthy era after Senator Joseph McCarthy, a zealous anti-Communist. Hundreds of people were hounded out of their jobs because of unfounded accusations of "Communist subversion," and many were required to testify before committees such as HUAC. Disney was an active participant in the anti-Communist movement at least as early as February 1944, when he became vice-president of the Motion Picture Alliance for the Preservation of American Ideals, whose Statement of Principles advocated freeing Hollywood of "domination by Communists, radicals, and crackpots." In a March 7, 1944, letter, the organization urged HUAC to investigate Hollywood, citing the "flagrant manner in which the motion picture industrialists of Hollywood have been coddling Communists and totalitarian-minded groups working in the industry for the dissemination of un-American ideas and beliefs." The ensuing investigation cast suspicions on virtually everyone involved in union organizing in Hollywood.

Walt Disney (center) samples the South American beverage yerba maté during his 1941 tour of the region.

Walt Disney testifies before the House Un-American Activities Committee (HUAC) on October 24, 1947. Disney, who had urged HUAC to investigate Hollywood, alleged that the leaders of the Disney strike were Communist subversives.

Despite his bitter feelings about the 1941 strike, Disney continued making animated films. *Dumbo,* released in late 1941, was intended as a low-budget feature that could offset some of the studio's financial setbacks. Relieved of the burden of attempting another revolutionary advance in animation, Disney's artists produced one of their most delightful and touching films. *Dumbo* was the first Disney feature since *Snow White and the Seven Dwarfs* to generate a profit.

A picture of Dumbo was scheduled to appear on the cover of *Time* magazine in December 1941, but the flying elephant was bumped from *Time* by aircraft of an entirely different kind. The Japanese air force bombed the U.S. naval base in Pearl Harbor, Hawaii, on December 7.

The changes at the Disney Studio were immediate. That very afternoon, Disney received a call at home that 500 soldiers had moved onto the Disney lot, which the army was commandeering as a repair base and ammunition storage center. The Disney studio—the only one so occupied—was abandoned by the army eight months later, when it became apparent that the Japanese were not going to invade Los Angeles.

After Pearl Harbor, various divisions of the U.S. government, including the army, navy, and the Department of Agriculture, asked Disney to produce animated training and propaganda films. The government work helped keep the studio in business during the war, as Disney had shelved all feature production and development. For the duration of the war, more than 90 percent of the Disney studio's production was war related.

One last feature of the Disney Golden Age—*Bambi*—was finally released in 1942. In development since 1937, this tale of a young deer's life in the forest had originally been intended to follow *Snow White*. Disney desired a lyrical, poetic yet naturalistic approach that could not be rushed. "It was a change of pace for us," Disney later explained. "With Bambi, there was a need for subtlety . . . for more of a life-like type of animation." To that end, Disney brought two live fawns to the studio so the artists could draw from life. He also hired nature photographers to film the flora and fauna of a Maine forest.

Disney encouraged his small handpicked crew of animators to achieve just the right balance of caricature and realism in the animal characters. When he saw test footage, animated by Frank Thomas and Milt Kahl, Disney was moved to tears. "Fellas, this is pure gold," he proudly told his artists.

Although it contains moments of comedy and song, *Bambi* is essentially a serious story, dealing with life and death; few who see *Bambi* ever forget the death of Bambi's mother by a hunter's bullet. Sadly, as was the case when *Pinocchio* was released, a world at war did not seem interested in the beautifully wrought animation of a Disney film. Another Disney masterpiece, another box office failure.

The war-themed cartoons produced by the studio were exceptionally powerful, including one of the most popular films produced during World War II: *Der Fuehrer's Face* (1943), an Academy Award–winning satire starring Donald Duck as a worker trapped in nightmarish "Nutziland."

Donald Duck was also drafted to star in *The New Spirit* (1943), a short designed to inspire taxpayers to help the war effort by paying their taxes on time. Produced in an astounding six weeks, the cartoon was seen by 60 million people, resulting in the most prompt tax payments ever. Unfortunately, this success story was soured when some members of Congress accused Walt Disney of being a war profiteer.

In 1943, Disney released an unusual commercial feature. *Victory Through Air Power* brought to life the principles spelled out in the book of the same name by Major Alexander de Seversky, a Russian pilot in World War I, who foresaw the key role bombers would play in future wars. Rushed through production in only 14 months, the propaganda film lost money for Disney but he did not regret producing it: "It was just something that I believed in, and for no other reason than that I did it." Winston Churchill was impressed with the film and made certain that President Franklin D. Roosevelt and his Joint Chiefs of Staff saw it. The film influenced the Allies' decision to incorporate sufficient air power on D day—June 6, 1944—the day on which Allied forces invaded France.

When the war ended in 1945, the Allies were victorious and so was much of Hollywood; the war years were among the most profitable in movie history. For Walt Disney Productions, it was a different story; Roy Disney termed the war "lost years" for the studio.

Disney was more than $4 million in debt. Walt and Roy argued heatedly over the next move for their beleaguered studio. Walt favored a return to feature production, a costly, risky step Roy adamantly opposed. Walt finally hit on the compromise concept of the package picture—features comprised of several cartoon shorts strung together. But his real solution was the diversification of his product, which, as Disney later explained, was not such a new idea:

> I knew the diversifying of the business would be the salvation of it. I tried that in the beginning, because I didn't want to be stuck with the Mouse. So I went into the Silly Symphonies. . . . The Symphonies led to the features, without the work I did in the Symphonies, I'd never have been prepared ever to tackle *Snow White.* . . . Now I wanted to go beyond even that; I wanted to go beyond the cartoon. Because the cartoon had narrowed itself down. I could make them either seven or eight minutes long or eighty minutes long. I tried the package things, where I put five or six together to make an eighty-minute feature. Now I needed to diversify further, and that meant live action.

Live action was quicker and cheaper than animation, and Disney had always been interested in filming and

To prepare for their work on *Bambi,* Disney artists made field trips into the forest, studied animal anatomy, and worked with live models. On June 14, 1944, artist Rico LeBrun (standing, front center) tutored a group of artists with the help of a live deer.

cameras. For his first real plunge into live action, Disney chose the Uncle Remus stories of Joel Chandler Harris. The tales of Br'er Rabbit would be told in animation—featuring, incidentally, Disney's best cartoon work since *Bambi*—but the bulk of *Song of the South* (1946), centering on Uncle Remus's friendship with a troubled little boy, would be a live-action period drama. Although a song from the movie, "Zip-a-Dee-Doo-Dah," won an Oscar in 1946, critics found the story heavy-handed. But Disney was committed to the live-action format. One of his artists stated that the moment Disney rode a camera crane, he knew the animators had lost Walt.

A few *Song of the South* scenes combined live action with animation, a process considerably improved since the days of the Alice Comedies. When Ub Iwerks reconciled with Walt and returned to the Disney Studio in the early 1940s, he spent the rest of his career working on technical processes such as the one that made the combination of live action and animation so convincing.

Disney's first all live-action picture was an adaptation of author Robert Louis Stevenson's 1883 swashbuckler, *Treasure Island,* produced in England with funds frozen because of postwar economic restrictions. *Treasure Island* was the first of a series of live-action costume dramas Disney filmed in Great Britain.

Disney made live-action films of quite a different sort with his *True-Life Adventure* nature series. Fascinated with wildlife film since shooting footage for *Bambi,* Disney hired husband and wife photographers Alfred and Elma Milotte to photograph animals in Alaska. He fashioned their footage of seals on the Pribilof Islands into the documentary *Seal Island.* As with Mickey Mouse and the *Silly Symphony* cartoons, distributors were not interested in this "True-Life Adventure," and Disney had to book the nature short himself. Once again, however, his prescience was confirmed when the film won an

Academy Award as Best Two-Reel Documentary of 1948. The series was launched, and Disney's *True-Life Adventures* racked up Oscars as his cartoons had done in the 1930s.

The various cartoon pastiches, however, had not performed well. Disney knew a return to full-fledged feature animation was crucial. He favored *Alice in Wonderland* as the first postwar feature, but Roy felt it lacked appeal. Disney turned to *Cinderella* for its many *Snow White*–like qualities.

If a feature were to be made, it had to be done quickly and with a minimum of costly changes. Disney decided to expand on the live-action reference film idea and make a prototype *Cinderella* motion picture. This live-action version would determine staging and timing before a single drawing had been made.

Though they saw the need for it, the Disney animators found this approach limiting; they felt that the live action, although only a guide, made their animation earthbound. Still, Disney's planning and the talents of his animators paid off; *Cinderella* was one of the biggest hits of 1950, the year Roy Disney called "our Cinderella year."

Roy was proved correct about *Alice in Wonderland*. Released in 1951, the adaptation of Lewis Carroll's surreal fantasy had flashes of brilliance but lacked the emotional involvement one usually associates with Disney's pictures; Walt himself acknowledged that *Alice* lacked "heart."

The failure of *Alice in Wonderland* was a setback for the studio. Fortunately, Disney's sure-handed animated adaptation of *Peter Pan* (1953) was a hit. But Walt, still struggling to get his studio to the point where its fortunes did not rise and fall on one picture, knew there was a bigger, better way to entertain his audience while assuring his studio of financial stability.

8 A Magic Kingdom

ONE OF WALT'S LIFELONG interests was railroads. In December 1947, Disney gave himself a gift—a shiny electric train. He set it up in his office and enjoyed showing it off to visitors, especially animators Ward Kimball and Ollie Johnston. They were even bigger railroad buffs than Walt: Kimball had a full-size railroad at his home, and Johnston was building a miniature train on his property.

Disney soon outgrew the novelty of the electric train in his office and decided to build his own miniature steam railroad. He and Lilly were looking for property to build a new house in Holmby Hills, and he made sure the lot was big enough to accommodate his homegrown railroad.

Disney planned the route of the tracks, the landscaping, and the building of the one-eighth-scale train itself with characteristic precision and thoroughness. In overalls and conductor's cap, Disney enjoyed giving rides to children and adults alike on his backyard train.

Walt Disney's personal railroad was part of the genesis of an idea that had been taking form in his fertile imagination for some time. As early as 1933,

Walt Disney pats a robotic rhino before its installation in Disneyland.

Disney had thought about creating an amusement park where people visiting Hollywood could have some fun and relaxation. In 1948, Disney outlined fairly detailed plans for an amusement park called Mickey Mouse Park to be built across the street from the Buena Vista Studio. Roy quickly reminded Walt of the escalating Disney debt whenever his brother mentioned the park idea.

But according to Walt, "Disneyland really began when my two daughters were very young. Saturday was always 'Daddy's Day' and I would take them to the merry-go-round and sit on a bench eating peanuts while they rode. And sitting there, alone, I felt that there should be something built, some kind of a family park where parents and children could have fun together."

Roy was steadfast in his opposition to the park. ". . . whenever I'd go down and talk to my brother about it," said Disney, "why, he'd always suddenly get busy with some figures so . . . I didn't dare bring it up. But I kept working on it and I worked on it with my own money." When Walt hocked his own life insurance to finance the initial planning of the park, it was Lilly's turn to object. ". . . my wife used to say, 'But why do you want to build an amusement park? They're so dirty,'" Disney later reported, "I told her that was just the point—mine wouldn't be."

To free himself of the constraints imposed by partners and stockholders, Disney formed his own company. Called WED Enterprises (Walter Elias Disney), it was staffed with artists who had long worked in animation. They understood Walt's creativity and his clear way of unambiguous cinematic storytelling. Most important, perhaps, they were used to giving Disney whatever he asked for, even if it was the impossible.

As quickly as his ideas and plans for this park multiplied, Disney's money ran out. If Disneyland, as Walt now called the park, was to become a reality, a way to finance the project had to be found. One sleepless night, Disney arrived at the answer to his financial quandary: television.

The Hollywood movie studios were fearful of television. The powerful new medium cut into film audiences as people stayed home to watch such TV programs as "I Love Lucy." TV was changing the face of the entertainment industry that the Hollywood movie colony had built and shaped to its own liking. Television was a distrusted interloper.

Walt Disney saw TV not as an enemy but as an ally. To him, TV was a goodwill ambassador, a way to let his audience know what he was doing. Disney had been the first major Hollywood figure to provide programming for television, having produced two Christmas specials in 1950 and 1951. Now he was ready to produce a weekly TV show for the networks, but at a price: whoever broadcast the Disney show had to invest in Disneyland.

Roy Disney liked the idea of a Disney television show; he even began to think that Disneyland could be a viable reality. But if Roy was to interest the TV networks in Disneyland, he would have to show them a design, a visual description. As yet, there was nothing on paper but the most preliminary of plans.

Walt met with Herb Ryman, a friend and former Disney artist, at the studio one Saturday morning in September 1953. Disney told Ryman about his grandiose idea and explained that Roy needed a visual of Disneyland to show to the networks in New York that Monday morning. Ryman agreed that such a drawing would be essential and asked Disney if he could see one. Walt told him there would only be a drawing of Disneyland when Ryman had drawn it.

Disney and Ryman worked all weekend on a schematic aerial view of the Magic Kingdom that existed only in Walt Disney's mind. On Monday, Roy flew to New

York with the picture and a description written by producer Bill
Walsh that put Walt's ideas on
paper for the first time: "The idea
of Disneyland is a simple one. It
will be a place for people to find
happiness and knowledge. . . . Disneyland will be something of a fair,
an exhibition, a playground, a
community center, a museum of
living facts, and a showplace of
beauty and magic."

In other words, Disneyland was
a brand new idea, a concept in
entertainment that would have to
be experienced to be believed.

In New York, Roy met with all
three networks, but it was the
American Broadcasting Corpora-
tion (ABC), then the smallest and
least significant of the TV networks, that was most anxious to
have the prestige and quality of a
Disney production. A deal was
struck: ABC would invest in Disneyland in return for a
weekly Disney TV show.

In April 1954, Walt Disney made his announcement:
Disneyland would open in July 1955. Now the time for
planning was aside. What was being called Walt Disney's
greatest dream—or, as *Snow White and the Seven Dwarfs*
had also been known two decades earlier, Disney's
Folly—had to become a reality made of concrete, asphalt,
and plywood in just over one year.

After a plan to build the park near the Disney Studio
in Burbank was abandoned because of lack of space,
Disney had commissioned the Stanford Research Insti-

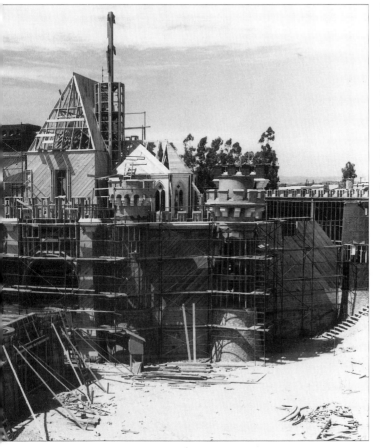

When Disney announced his plan to build his unprecedented theme park in April 1954, he promised that it would open to the public in July 1955, leaving barely more than a year to complete construction. Building crews worked frantically right up until the July 17 deadline, and Disneyland opened on schedule.

tute to find the best location for his park, and their findings indicated that the pleasant climate, available land, and a soon-to-be-constructed freeway made Anaheim, California, the most desirable locale. Disney also consulted amusement park owners for their opinion of the Disneyland project. Their response was unanimous: Save your money, forget the whole thing, it will never work. Disney went ahead exactly as he had planned.

Whenever anyone called Disneyland an amusement park, Disney quickly corrected their error: Disneyland was not an amusement park but what would become known as a theme park, a whole new concept. Carefully planned attractions would be designed around a central idea expressed in every detail. Even the wastebaskets would be thematic with appropriate colors and graphics. Everything would be designed for the comfort and entertainment of the customers, or "guests," as Walt insisted on calling those who would come to experience Disneyland.

Disneyland was designed by artists and designers— Imagineers, Disney dubbed them—who used their experience in animation and motion pictures to make each

Instead of the 15,000 invited guests, 33,000 people, many with counterfeit tickets, showed up for Disneyland's July 17, 1955, opening day. Although there were initially a number of problems with the park, which was not yet totally completed—the asphalt on Main Street was still hot, for example, causing women's high-heeled shoes to sink into it—within seven weeks 1,000,000 people had visited the park.

part of Fantasyland, Tomorrowland, Frontierland, and Adventureland in Disneyland a story. But unlike at the movies, Disneyland's guests would not be passive spectators but active participants in the story.

At the various fairs, parks, and museums Disney had visited throughout the world, he found the attractions and exhibits laid out in a hodgepodge manner that required too much walking through mazelike streets. Disneyland, he told his Imagineers, would have "a single entrance through which all traffic would flow, then a

hub off which the various areas [will be] situated. That gives people a sense of orientation—they know where they are at all times. And it saves a lot of walking." Moreover, the many attractions would not clash or cancel each other out; they would be designed as a harmonious whole, with one area flowing into the next through the use of color and architecture, leading to a feeling of pleasant satisfaction rather than fatigued confusion.

A fanciful landscape sprang up in Anaheim. Where once orange trees had stood row by row, now there appeared a steamboat, a rocket, jungles and rivers, and a fairy-tale castle. A 20-foot earthen berm surrounded this burgeoning Magic Kingdom, keeping out the real world. "I don't want the public to see the world they live in while they're in the Park," Disney stated. "I want them to feel they're in another world." The Disneyland Railroad, based on Walt's backyard train, would chug along atop the berm. Considering Disney's love for trains and his railroad experience, it is not surprising that the Disneyland Railroad was one of the first attractions to be completed.

The year 1954 was a busy one for Disney. His eldest daughter Diane married Ron Miller, a football player she had met while attending the University of Southern California (USC). Both Walt and Lilly were fond of

Vice-president Richard M. Nixon visits the newly opened Disneyland theme park with his family .

Miller, and though he played tight end for USC, Disney convinced him to come work at the studio, and eventually he became a producer. Sharon Disney married Bob Brown in 1959. He, too, soon joined the Disney organization as a planner at WED. The Millers ultimately gave Walt seven grandchildren; Sharon and Bob Brown had a daughter in 1966.

The "Disneyland" TV series premiered in 1954 with Walt Disney himself serving as host. There could not have been a better choice; Disney was comfortable, welcoming, and, to none of his animators' surprise, a good

Fess Parker (left) sings for Walt Disney (center) and director Norman Foster. The three-part "Davy Crockett" TV series starring Parker set off a national craze; millions of children bought coonskin caps, and the "Ballad of Davy Crocket" became the number one song in America for 13 weeks.

Sharon Disney Brown receives a kiss from her father, Walt Disney, and her husband, Robert Brown (right), on her wedding day in May 1959.

performer. The first episode of "Disneyland" was dedicated to a preview of the park, coming attractions of the TV show, and a salute to Mickey Mouse. "I hope we never lose sight of one thing," said Disney, even as he unveiled his most ambitious plans " . . . that this was all started by a Mouse." A few weeks later "Disneyland" caused an immense national craze when it broadcast "Davy Crockett" in three weekly installments. Millions of children placed coonskin caps on their heads—more than 10 million hats were sold in all—and a song from the show, the "Ballad of Davy Crockett," topped the music charts for 13 weeks. To ABC's delight, "Disneyland" became the number one show on television.

Spring 1955 found the scheduled July 17 opening of Disneyland looming ever closer. Tomorrowland was incomplete, and there was no way to finish it in time. Disney briefly considered not opening the area but then simply instructed that Tomorrowland be covered with balloons and pennants. Money was running low, and the landscaping was not finished. "You know all those fancy Latin names for plants," Disney told his landscaper, Bill Evans. "Why don't you go down there and put some Latin names on those weeds." On his weekly show Disney kept his millions of TV viewers posted on the progress of the park. And on July 17, 1955, millions tuned in to a special called "Dateline Disneyland," covering the grand opening of Walt Disney's brand new, $17 million Magic Kingdom. Viewers of the TV special were unaware that Opening Day was a nightmare of glitches and snafus. The grand opening was by invitation only, but someone had counterfeited tickets. Disneyland was surrounded by a traffic jam that congested a 10-mile radius as 33,000 people swarmed into the just-barely-completed park. Rides broke down; food and drink ran out; Fantasyland was closed because of a gas leak; high-heeled shoes stuck in the asphalt softened by the hot sun; and the *Mark Twain* steamboat listed when too many people crowded onto its decks.

Disney spent the next two weeks at Disneyland, working 24 hours a day with his team to correct all the misfires of the day he would ever after refer to as Black Sunday.

But if Opening Day was less than perfect, the days that followed more than made up for it. In just seven weeks, 1 million guests had visited Disneyland.

The World of Tomorrow

"**A**LMOST EVERYONE WARNED US that Disneyland would be a Hollywood spectacular—a spectacular failure," said Walt Disney. Instead, Disneyland was a spectacular success. It was his greatest triumph, a place where millions of Disney fans could come and stay and play. Disney loved being at the park with the young and old who came to experience this revolutionary concept in entertainment. He just stood and watched them. "Have you ever seen so many happy people?" he would say, beaming. Disney liked spending time in the park so much that he had an apartment built directly above the fire station on Disneyland's Main Street.

Walt Disney Productions now had a steady source of revenue, but the success of Disneyland did not mean that Disney neglected his other arenas. The "Disneyland" TV series continued, and in 1955, he came up with the idea for a children's TV program, the first Disney production ever made exclusively for children.

"The Mickey Mouse Club" starred 24 talented boys and girls called the Mouseketeers. They wore mouse-ear hats, based on a gag in an old Mickey

Walt Disney drives a fire engine around Disneyland, accompanied by his protégé, Mickey Mouse.

Mouse cartoon where Mickey tipped his ears to Minnie. Mickey Mouse himself introduced the show as millions of children tuned in every day for an hour to see the classic Disney cartoons and the bubbly Mouseketeers—in particular Annette Funicello, who became the most popular of the Mouseketeers.

Disney's animators produced the first 3-D cartoon, *Adventures in Music: Melody,* in 1953. *Toot, Whistle, Plunk, and Boom* (1953), which won yet another Oscar for Disney, was the first cartoon to be made in Cinema-Scope, a wide-screen format developed to counter the threat of television. In 1955, *Lady and the Tramp* became the first animated feature made in CinemaScope.

Disney planned his next feature, *Sleeping Beauty,* to be in the even wider wide-screen process of Technirama 70; he envisioned it as the pinnacle of the art of animation. Artist Eyvind Earle designed *Sleeping Beauty* in the style of Renaissance paintings and medieval tapestries. *Sleeping Beauty's* soundtrack, with music adapted from the Tchaikovsky ballet, was recorded in stereophonic sound.

The feature's rigid stylization made for beautiful images but a rather cold, uninvolving story. The characters are all well animated but they distance the viewer rather than engage his or her emotions. The character of Sleeping Beauty in particular invokes little audience response, especially when compared to Snow White or Cinderella. At $6 million, *Sleeping Beauty* was Disney's most expensive feature, but it failed at the box office.

With Disneyland a firmly established success, however, the studio was on solid financial ground. Disney was spared the worry and pressure of financial woes. Disneyland finally made Walt Disney what most people assumed he had always been: a wealthy man. He was driving home one day when he saw a Mercedes-Benz in a showroom window. Wistfully wishing he could afford the "jazzy little sports car," he drove on. It was only after driving a few blocks that Disney realized he could afford the car. He turned around, went back to the showroom, and bought the car then and there.

"Disneyland will never be completed," Disney was fond of saying. "It will continue to grow as long as there is imagination left in the world." Disney never tired of improving, or "plussing," Disneyland. He felt Tomorrowland had been neglected, and in 1959, he implemented a $6 million face-lift, adding the Submarine Voyage and a state-of-the-art monorail system. Disneyland's Matterhorn replica was constructed, adding another unusual feature to the Anaheim skyline.

Disneyland's Jungle Cruise and Nature's Wonderland attractions featured model animals that moved with simple motions, but Disney wanted more complex figures. His long fascination with models, miniatures, and mechanical figures came to the forefront as Disney told his Imagineers he wanted to animate three-dimensional figures just as he had brought drawings to life in his cartoons. They developed Audio-Animatronics—"sound and animation through electronics," as Disney explained it. "The tape sends signals and the little figures work and they sing and act and move according to the impulse that comes from the tape. And this is all possible because of this big drive that we've had on the space age development, the electronic age."

Disney's first application of Audio-Animatronics was at a Disneyland attraction, the Enchanted Tiki Room, which featured birds, tiki gods, and flowers singing and telling jokes. But Disney had a much more ambitious project in mind: a moving, speaking Abraham Lincoln.

A World's Fair was being planned for New York in 1964. Disney offered to create exhibits for the participating corporations, knowing that the sponsors' money would develop ideas and technology to benefit Disney in the future.

Disney contracted to create exhibits with Ford, the state of Illinois, General Electric, and Pepsi-Cola. Pepsi wanted an attraction to benefit the United Nations International Children's Emergency Fund (UNICEF). The resulting ride wound through colorful doll-like figures of children from around the world dressed in their native costumes. But it needed a song. Disney challenged his staff songwriters, Richard and Robert Sherman, to write a song that could be sung in any language with any instrumentation, simultaneously. The Sherman brothers, whose first work for Disney was writing songs for Annette Funicello, came up with one of the most famous Disney tunes, "It's a Small World."

Work progressed on the World's Fair Exhibits and the experimental Abraham Lincoln prototype. Walt Disney later related what happened next:

> I figured it would take me 10 years to get Mr. Lincoln going. . . . We could make him stand up and put his hand out. Robert Moses [president of the New York World's Fair] . . . wanted to visit the studio. He was trying to get ideas on what could be done. So I had him meet Abraham Lincoln. I said, "Would you like to meet Mr. Lincoln?" He gave me a funny look. I said, "well come on in—meet him." So when he walked in the door, I said, "Mr. Lincoln meet Mr. Moses," and Lincoln stood up and put his hand out and Moses went over and shook hands with him. Well, Moses is quite a showman and he said I've got to have Lincoln in the Fair. But I said this is 5 years away anyway. But Moses wouldn't take no for an answer. The next thing I knew he had gotten with the state of Illinois and was trying to sell them on a Pavilion. And before I knew it I had my arm twisted and I said yes. We now had to get Mr. Lincoln on the road, I think, in about 13 months.

As the Imagineers struggled to perfect the Lincoln figure, Disney weathered criticism that he was turning the revered president into a cartoon; others wondered if

The talking, moving model of Abraham Lincoln devised by Disney's Imagineers was a favorite attraction at the 1964 World's Fair in New York City and later became a fixture in Disneyland.

Disney should even be creating a human figure, especially Lincoln, and considered it crass and in poor taste. The Disney reputation was on the line.

The four Disney exhibits—Great Moments with Mr. Lincoln, Carousel of Progress, Magic Skyway, and It's a Small World—were shipped to New York, along with 200 WED employees. They got Mr. Lincoln on his feet and he suddenly starting convulsing, smashing chairs, and in general acting in a most unpresidential manner.

Dignitaries from the state of Illinois and the press gathered for a preview of Great Moments with Mr. Lincoln, but for the first time in his professional career, Walt Disney missed a deadline. Mr. Lincoln simply was not ready, Disney himself told the preview audience, and Walt would not open the exhibit until he was. One week later, after the opening of the World's Fair, Mr. Lincoln began functioning perfectly. The Illinois Pavilion opened and became one of the favorite attractions of the Fair, as did the other Disney exhibits.

In 1964, Disney released a film that was a summation of his entire career: *Mary Poppins*. As Disney explained it:

> After a long concentration on live-action and cartoon films, we decided to try something that would employ about every trick we had learned in the making of films. We would combine cartoon and live-action in an enormous fantasy—*Mary Poppins*. . . . As the original *Mary Poppins* budget of five million dollars continued to grow, I never saw a sad face around the entire studio. And this made me nervous. I knew the picture would have to gross ten million dollars for us to break even. But still there was no negative head-shaking. No prophets of doom. Even Roy was happy. He didn't even ask me to show the unfinished picture to a banker. The horrible thought struck me—suppose the staff had finally conceded that I knew what I was doing.

The genesis of *Mary Poppins* began in 1939, when Disney discovered his daughter Diane laughing over one of the Poppins books by P. L. Travers. Diane explained to her father that Mary Poppins was a prim and very magical nanny. Intrigued with the filmic possibilities, Disney began negotiations with the author; however, it was not until 1960 that the rather eccentric and quite particular Mrs. Travers sold Disney the movie rights.

Disney cast Julie Andrews, then Broadway's favorite musical star, as Mary Poppins. The Sherman brothers composed the songs, including the ballad "Feed the Birds," which became Walt's favorite of all the Disney songs, and "Chim Chim Cheree," which won an Academy Award. *Mary Poppins* was a phenomenal hit; it was the most popular film of Disney's career. Critics raved, calling the musical-fantasy "one of the most magnificent pieces of entertainment ever to come from Hollywood." Julie Andrews won an Academy Award as Best Actress of 1964. "Mr. Walt Disney gets the biggest thanks," she said as she accepted her Oscar.

At the time of *Mary Poppins,* few suspected Disney was planning a new theme park. He had seriously considered an Eastern Disneyland as early as 1958. But a Magic Kingdom would only be one part of a vast complex, an entire Disney World. Three surveys pegged Orlando, Florida, as the best location, and Disney secretly began buying up property, eventually purchasing a block of land twice the size of the island of Manhattan. Disney

Julie Andrews won an Academy Award in 1964 for her performance in the title role of *Mary Poppins,* one of Disney's most popular and imaginative feature films.

regretted how the area surrounding Disneyland had become a "second-rate Las Vegas" because he could not afford more land; now he said, "There's enough land here to hold all the ideas and plans we can possibly imagine."

His most exciting new idea was a City of Tomorrow, a planned community that became Disney's magnificent obsession. He had no patience with talk about the Magic Kingdom, even though that would be the first phase constructed; Disney already knew how to build a Disneyland. Instead, he talked and dreamed constantly about his city, reading books on city planning and consulting with industry leaders and city planners.

As Disney continued to pour his energies into the Florida project, Roy started talking about retirement. He was in his seventies and wanted to enjoy more time with his family. To Walt, the idea was unthinkable; he needed Roy to bring Disney World and the City of Tomorrow to life, as surely as he had needed him to start the studio in 1923. Roy reluctantly agreed to put off his retirement.

In October 1966, Disney announced his new idea, which he called EPCOT, short for Experimental Prototype Community of Tomorrow. He explained, "It will be a community of tomorrow that will never be completed but will always be introducing and teaching and demonstrating new materials and systems. And EPCOT will be a showcase to the world for the ingenuity and imagination of American free enterprise."

After *Sleeping Beauty*'s expensive failure, Disney considered disbanding the animation department completely, but he felt a debt of gratitude toward the artists who had loyally helped build his company. As he had in the early days, Ub Iwerks came to the rescue of Disney animation. He developed a system using the new Xerox photocopying technology to mechanically copy the animators' drawings onto the cels, thus eliminating the costly step of inking the drawings by hand. The new process was successfully used in the fresh, contemporary story *101 Dalmatians,* which was released in 1961 and became a hit.

The Jungle Book seemed to revive Disney's personal involvement in animation. Disney immersed himself in the story meetings with a vigor his artists had not seen since the days of the early features. "You guys ought to have me down here more often," quipped Disney. "I'm the least-paid gag man in the studio." When the animators and story artists were having trouble creating the character of Baloo the Bear, Disney suggested the slangy, gravel-voiced bandleader Phil Harris—and acted out how Harris seemed to be always moving to a beat. Harris's voice and Disney's dance were the keys to the character; Baloo's role was expanded and the bear became the star of the picture. Released in 1967, 30 years after *Snow White and the Seven Dwarfs, The Jungle Book* was an enormous success, reaffirming the potency of the animated art form Disney had played such a major role in developing.

By 1966, people all over the world recognized the name "Disney" as meaning a particular amusing and involving kind of family entertainment. Walt was protective of the Disney image; he wanted nothing and nobody to detract from the image that had been built up over the years.

In the 1930s, Mickey Mouse had become somewhat limited as a character because of his good guy image. If he did anything even remotely mischievous, Disney received letters of complaint. Over the years, Walt Disney himself had become something of a prisoner of the Disney image. He sometimes wished he could make a more serious, challenging sort of film, such as *To Kill a Mockingbird,* the dramatic 1962 film about racial prejudice, but he knew the Disney audience would not accept it.

Disney felt that his own life no longer fit the image he had created; "I'm not Walt Disney anymore," he would say. He drank, swore, and smoked, all behavior he deemed inappropriate for the Disney image.

Smoking was a particular problem for him. For years, Disney had been warned to give up the cigarettes he chain-smoked, but it seemed impossible. The lit cigarette he always held seemed to be an extension of his hand, the smoking part of his intense energy.

In late 1966, X rays divulged a large spot on his left lung. Disney drove himself to St. Joseph's Hospital, across the street from the studio, on the day of the surgery. He told Lilly and his daughters there was no need to be there. The Disney women did come, of course, and the news was bad: The lung was cancerous and had been removed. Walt Disney was given six months to two years to live.

It was impossible for Lilly and the Disney daughters to comprehend. Walt had always been energetic and full of life. Weak and gaunt, Disney did leave the hospital, and he spent several days at the studio and WED, checking on film production and receiving an update on the new, yet to be opened Disneyland attraction, Pirates of the Caribbean. But just over a week later, he was back in the hospital. He spent his last days still imagining, still planning the Disney World project on the foot-square acoustical tiles on the ceiling above his bed.

On December 15, 1966, just 10 days after his 65th birthday, Walt Disney died.

He had kept the seriousness of his illness secret, and many of his co-workers at Walt Disney Productions were shocked when they heard about it. The entire world mourned his loss, with newspapers around the globe publishing obituaries; more than one publication printed a drawing of a weeping Mickey Mouse. The *New York Times* observed:

A cartoon by Don Wright of the *Miami News* shows Walt Disney's beloved creations mourning Disney's death from lung cancer in 1966.

He had a genius for innovation; his production was enormous; he was able to keep sure and personal control over his increasingly far-flung enterprise; his hand was ever on the public pulse. He was, in short, a legend in his own lifetime—and so honored many times over. Yet none of this sums up Walt Disney.

Some thought that the Disney World project would collapse without Walt, but Roy Disney was determined

Participants in the charity event Hands Across America join hands in front of Disneyland's Sleeping Beauty Castle in 1986.

to bring the project to fruition as Walt had planned it. He once again postponed retirement to personally handle the Florida project's financing and oversee its completion before opening day. Roy also formally announced that the official title of the Florida theme park would be Walt Disney World, "so people will always know that this was Walt's dream."

On October 1, 1971, Walt Disney World had its spectacular opening day. Roy Disney, with Mickey Mouse at his side, proudly stepped before the microphone and addressed the thousands present and the millions watching on TV: "My brother Walt and I first went into business together almost a half-century ago. And he was really, in my opinion, truly a genius."

Roy had succeeded in making Walt's vision for the first phase of Walt Disney World a reality. "My job all along was to help Walt to do the things he wanted to do," Roy said simply. "He did the dreaming; I did the building."

On December 20, 1971, only three months after dedicating Walt Disney World to the memory of his younger brother, Roy Disney died.

EPCOT Center opened at Walt Disney World on October 1, 1982. It was a modified version of Walt Disney's concept of a prototype community. No one could quite figure out how to make the City of Tomorrow concept a working reality, and without Disney's inspiration, the ambitious plans to create a fully functioning model community where innovations and improvements in urban life could be demonstrated never materialized.

Today, with Tokyo Disneyland and Euro Disneyland, in addition to Walt Disney World and Disneyland, the sun literally never sets on the Disney empire. The Disney legacy of animation lives on in a new generation of animators, many trained by Walt's veteran artists. *Beauty and the Beast* (1991) was the first animated feature to be honored with an Academy Award nomination for Best Picture, and *Aladdin* became the most successful Disney movie of all time within a year of its release in 1992. A rocky first year for Euro Disney—the French-based theme park and hotel complex lost $900,000,000 in its opening season—did not slow planning for a proposed new park near Washington, D.C., that will feature attractions based on American history.

Walt Disney's creativity is an enduring legacy. Never content to simply repeat what he had done before, he always instilled a fresh, inventive spirit in everything he did. In 1964, Lyndon B. Johnson gave Walt Disney the nation's highest civilian honor, the Medal of Freedom. The citation read: "Artist and impresario, in the course of entertaining an age Walt Disney has created an American folklore."

Appendix ★★★★★★★★★★★★★★★★★★★★★★

Walt Disney's Feature Films, 1937–67

A comprehensive list of the feature films produced by the Disney Studio during Walt Disney's lifetime.

Snow White and the Seven Dwarfs (1937)
Pinocchio (1940)
Fantasia (1940)
The Reluctant Dragon (1941)
Dumbo (1941)
Bambi (1942)
Saludos Amigos (1943)
Victory Through Air Power (1943)
The Three Caballeros (1945)
Make Mine Music (1946)
Song of the South (1946)
Fun & Fancy Free (1947)
Melody Time (1948)
So Dear to My Heart (1949)
The Adventures of Ichabod and Mr. Toad (1949)
Cinderella (1950)
Treasure Island (1950)
Alice in Wonderland (1951)
The Story of Robin Hood (1952)
Peter Pan (1953)
The Sword and the Rose (1953)
The Living Desert (1953)
Rob Roy, the Highland Rogue (1954)
The Vanishing Prairie (1954)
20,000 Leagues Under the Sea (1954)
Davy Crockett, King of the Wild Frontier (1955)
Lady and the Tramp (1955)
The African Lion (1955)
The Littlest Outlaw (1955)
The Great Locomotive Chase (1956)
Davy Crockett and the River Pirates (1956)
Secrets of Life (1956)
Westward Ho the Wagons! (1956)
Johnny Tremain (1957)
Perri (1957)
Old Yeller (1957)
The Light in the Forest (1958)
White Wilderness (1958)
Tonka (1958)
Sleeping Beauty (1959)
The Shaggy Dog (1959)
Darby O'Gill and the Little People (1959)
Third Man on the Mountain (1959)

Toby Tyler, or Ten Weeks with a Circus (1960)
Kidnapped (1960)
Pollyanna (1960)
Jungle Cat (1960)
Ten Who Dared (1960)
Swiss Family Robinson (1960)
The Sign of Zorro (1960)
One Hundred and One Dalmations (1961)
The Absent Minded Professor (1961)
The Parent Trap (1961)
Nikki, Wild Dog of the North (1961)
Greyfriars Bobby (1961)
Babes in Toyland (1961)
Moon Pilot (1962)
Bon Voyage! (1962)
Big Red (1962)
Almost Angels (1962)
The Legend of Lobo (1962)
In Search of the Castaways (1962)
Son of Flubber (1963)
Miracle of the White Stallions (1963)
Savage Sam (1963)
Summer Magic (1963)
The Incredible Journey (1963)
The Sword in the Stone (1963)
The Misadventures of Merlin Jones (1964)
A Tiger Walks (1964)
The Three Lives of Thomasina (1964)
The Moon-Spinners (1964)
Mary Poppins (1964)
Emil and the Detectives (1964)
Those Calloways (1965)
The Monkey's Uncle (1965)
That Darn Cat! (1965)
The Ugly Dachshund (1965)
Lt. Robin Crusoe USN (1966)
The Fighting Prince of Donegal (1966)
Follow Me, Boys! (1966)
Monkeys, Go Home! (1967)
The Adventures of Bullwhip Griffin (1967)
The Gnome-Mobile (1967)
The Jungle Book (1967)
The Happiest Millionaire (1967)

Further Reading ★ ★ ★ ★ ★ ★ ★ ★ ★ ★ ★ ★ ★ ★ ★

Culhane, John. *Walt Disney's Fantasia.* New York: Harry N. Abrams, 1983.

Eliot, Marc. *Walt Disney: Hollywood's Dark Prince.* New York: Birch Lane Press, 1993.

Finch, Christopher. *The Art of Walt Disney: From Mickey Mouse to the Magic Kingdoms.* New York: Harry N. Abrams, 1973.

Johnston, Ollie, and Frank Thomas. *Walt Disney's Bambi: The Story and the Film.* New York: Stewart, Tabori & Chang, 1990.

Maltin, Leonard. *The Disney Films.* Updated edition. New York: Crown Publishers, 1984.

Miller, Diane Disney, as told to Pete Martin. *The Story of Walt Disney.* New York: Holt, 1957.

Solomon, Charles. *Enchanted Drawings: The History of Animation.* New York: Alfred A. Knopf, 1989.

Thomas, Bob. *Walt Disney: An American Original.* New York: Simon & Schuster, 1976.

Thomas, Frank, and Ollie Johnston. *Disney Animation: The Illusion of Life.* New York: Abbeville Press, 1981.

Chronology ★ ★ ★ ★ ★ ★ ★ ★ ★ ★ ★ ★ ★ ★ ★ ★

1901   Born Walter Elias Disney on December 5 in Chicago, Illinois

1918   Goes to France with Red Cross Ambulance Corps

1919   Hired by Kansas City Slide Company; first professional job as artist; forms Laugh-O-gram Films with Ub Iwerks

1923   Arrives in Hollywood, California; Signs contract with M. J. Winkler to produce series of Alice Comedies on October 16 (this date is considered the start of the Disney studio)

1925   Marries Lillian Bounds on July 13

1926   Moves to studio on Hyperion Avenue

1927   Creates Oswald the Lucky Rabbit

1928   Creates character of Mickey Mouse; *Steamboat Willie,* first cartoon with fully synchronized sound, premieres in New York City on November 18

1929   *The Skeleton Dance,* the first *Silly Symphony,* is released

1932   *Flowers and Trees,* the first cartoon in full color and Disney's first Academy Award winner, is released; Disney art school founded at studio to train animators

1933   *Three Little Pigs* is released; song "Who's Afraid of the Big Bad Wolf?" becomes a number one hit

1934   *The Wise Little Hen,* with first appearance of Donald Duck, is released

1935   *The Band Concert,* first Mickey Mouse cartoon in color, is released

1937   *Snow White and the Seven Dwarfs,* first full-length animated feature, premieres

1940   *Pinocchio* is released; move to new studio in Burbank is completed; *Fantasia* is released

★ ★

1941	Unionization strike; Walt and artists embark on goodwill tour of South America; *Dumbo* is released; the U.S. Army moves onto Disney lot
1942	*Bambi* is released
1948	*Seal Island,* the first *True-Life Adventure,* is released
1950	*Treasure Island,* Disney's first completely live-action feature, is released; *Cinderella* is released; first television show, "One Hour in Wonderland," is broadcast
1951	*Alice in Wonderland* is released
1952	WED Enterprises is founded
1953	*Peter Pan* is released; *The Living Desert,* first feature-length *True-Life Adventure*, becomes the first picture distributed by Disney's Buena Vista Distribution Company
1954	"Disneyland" weekly TV series premieres; *20,000 Leagues Under the Sea* is released
1955	Disneyland opens in Anaheim, California; "The Mickey Mouse Club" TV series premieres
1959	*Sleeping Beauty* is released
1963	Enchanted Tiki Room, featuring first use of Audio-Animatronics, opens at Disneyland
1964	Four Disney exhibits open at the New York World's Fair, including Great Moments with Mr. Lincoln and It's a Small World; *Mary Poppins* is released
1966	Walt Disney dies on December 15
1971	Walt Disney World opens in Orlando, Florida; Roy Disney dies
1982	EPCOT Center opens at Walt Disney World

Index ★★★★★★★★★★★★★★★★★★★★★★★

Jim Fanning is the author of *The Disney Poster: The Animated Film Classics from Mickey Mouse to Aladdin* (1993). He has written numerous nationally published articles about Walt Disney and his works, including "Mickey Mouse's 60th Birthday" for *Cartoon Quarterly* magazine (1988) and "Horror in Disney Animation" for *Animato* magazine (1994). He also wrote many episodes of the Disney Channel television documentary series *Disney Family Album*. Fanning lives in Burbank, California.

Leeza Gibbons is a reporter for and cohost of the nationally syndicated television program "Entertainment Tonight" and NBC's daily talk show "John & Leeza from Hollywood." A graduate of the University of South Carolina's School of Journalism, Gibbons joined the on-air staff of "Entertainment Tonight" in 1984 after cohosting WCBS-TV's "Two on the Town" in New York City. Prior to that, she cohosted "PM Magazine" on WFAA-TV in Dallas, Texas, and on KFDM-TV in Beaumont, Texas. Gibbons also hosts the annual "Miss Universe," "Miss U.S.A.," and "Miss Teen U.S.A." pageants, as well as the annual Hollywood Christmas Parade. She is active in a number of charities and has served as the national chairperson for the Spinal Muscular Atrophy Division of the Muscular Dystrophy Association; each September, Gibbons cohosts the National MDA Telethon with Jerry Lewis.